THE PARAKEET DRAWING

YOU ARE WORTHY

GINA DEFA

with
LAUREN ECKHARDT

This is a work of creative nonfiction. These are the events and timeline as I remember them. There are chunks of time in which I have no memory and have done my best to lay out the events as chronologically as possible. In some cases, I have compressed multiple events into one. Some names that I no longer remember have been replaced. It is a book of memory, my memory. I have done my best to tell it truthfully.

Cover Design: Michelle Young
Professional Photographs: Front Street Photography

Burning Soul Press LLC
All rights reserved.
ISBN: 978-1-950476-18-3 Paperback

My dad. For always being my rock. My safe place. My daughters. You have healed me. I am forever thankful God trusted your beautiful souls to me.

This book was written to inspire men and women who have experienced trauma. You can heal. And you can do amazing things, all because of the journey you have been on.

PROLOGUE

*T*he first time I was asked to share my story, I was forty-four years old. I was a participant in the Multicultural Leadership Program (MCLP), a community-based servant leadership program in Bloomington-Normal, Illinois. As part of the curriculum, students shared their inspirational stories, something in their lives that had inspired them. When the facilitator announced the assignment, I immediately knew I was supposed to share the story of the parakeet drawing. I also immediately knew there was *no way* I was going to do that. By the end of class that day, we needed to sign up for a date to share our stories sometime during the nine-month program. Looking at the board, I signed up for a date in November. It was August, so I felt I bought myself a little time to decide what I would share. Walking out of the building, I heard God say, "It's time to share your story." To which I said, "No, no God, it's not. I can't."

During the months I had until it would be my turn to share, I went back and forth with God. You see, by sharing the story about the drawing, I would have to share the story about me. My mom. Jack. An overview of how we got to the place of the drawing that changed my life. People would be uncomfortable. I knew who I was and how my story had shaped me, but they didn't know those things. They saw whom they wanted to see; I didn't want to make them uncomfortable with the truth.

The night before I was to share my story, I was sitting on my bed writing it out. Well, trying to write it out. My hand shook and the words weren't flowing smoothly. I was saying too much or not enough. If it were too much, the class would feel awkward. If it were not enough, the class would not understand the impact of the drawing. I tried one last time, only to crumple up the paper and throw it on my bed with the other balls of failed attempts in writing it out. I took a deep breath and told God "no" one last time, while trying to come up with something else to share. I had to tell the class something, now what would it be?

Just then, my daughter Alissa came into my room and plopped on my bed. She was sad and needed to talk. This was unusual for Alissa. She didn't share much and she certainly wasn't down often. Alissa is an artist, and we had a running joke about the parakeet drawing. Her entire life when she painted, drew, or sketched out a beautiful piece of art, I would ensure she knew she got her talent from me, and I would proceed to draw the parakeet to prove it to her. She would laugh and say, "Mom, that is the only thing you can draw...I didn't get it from you." My daughters didn't know the meaning of the drawing. I had never shared it. They just knew I drew it.

"Mom, it's been a bad day," Alissa confessed.

"Why Lis? What happened?" *Yes! No more thinking about this silly sharing session tomorrow. I'm going to be a mom right*

*now and love on Alissa. I'll figure out what I'm going to share
with my class later.*

"I don't want to talk about it. I just came in here to ask if
you could draw the parakeet for me? It always makes me
feel better. I feel peaceful when you draw it."

I sighed. *Okay, God. Fine. I give in.*

I'll share the story tomorrow.

PART I

1

I AM OKAY

1989

"*A*re you fatter than me?" my mom's gravelly voice said through the phone.

I froze, the phone cord wrapped around my fingers, regretting answering the phone. She would call only a few times a year, and this was her customary greeting. Another drunk dial. The truth of what was between us hung in the air. She never wanted me skinnier than her. Or prettier than her. Or happier than her. A one-sided competitive dance between mother and her daughter, one I didn't engage in because I thought we should be on the same team.

But we never were.

I have often closed my eyes and tried to remember memories of my mom before things turned. I don't remember her hugging me or taking care of me at any point in my life. Even those important times like having the chicken pox or when I fell off a minibike and burned my leg, it was my dad's sisters who came to my rescue. My mom is removed from the scenes of those stories, a peripheral character. Always in the background. Always looking away.

Those are my memories. Her turning her head time and again. Sitting only inches away as vile acts happened to her only daughter, she turned her head.

While she didn't take care of me, I tried to take care of her. A little girl holding her mother's hair back as she vomited a mix of pills and alcohol in the toilet, her dentures falling into the hole, and me having to stick my arm in the warm water to fish them out. Getting called to the principal's office year after year, being handed the phone, my mom on the other end telling me she was in the hospital again and needed me to go home and pack her nightgown and robe for someone to take to her. Within a few days, she'd be back home as if nothing happened and as unresponsive to me as ever.

I remember walking into the apartment after school and seeing her on the floor, naked and lying in vomit with Jack yelling at me to clean her up. Being awoken in the middle of the night to her crying, of walking down the hallway in the apartment to find her as naked as the men who were around her.

Memories no child should ever have.

Especially not of their mom.

I was forced to watch her darkest times as she allowed her darkness to move over me, seizing the vulnerability of an innocent child.

"Are you ugly now?" Mom's voice drew me back to the phone pressed against my ear.

I closed my eyes, imagining the fetid smell of bourbon and smoke on her breath as if it were seeping through the phone and rubbed my swollen belly, confident that when this baby was born, I would protect her, elevate her, and love her at all costs.

Most moms would.

But not mine.

In this moment, I fully comprehended what she was to me, our relationship, the life she put me through. I realized I needed to take care of myself, my marriage, my job, and this new life that I was responsible for.

I couldn't keep doing this dance with her.

Before mom could ask me another question, I spoke my truth. I told her she could no longer call and abuse me. I told her that I love her and when she was ready to get clean, she could call me then, and I would help her. But until she was ready to do that, not to call me again.

I hung up the phone, summoning silence, distance, and years between her demons and my heart.

I reached for a pen and lost myself in the motions that came so naturally now. The pen's orchestrated dance on the paper, each mark connecting, slowly bringing to life a parakeet that caught my tears one by one as they dripped off my face. *I am okay,* I repeated over and over in my mind, willing myself to recapture my peace as I scratched the paper with the tip. *I am enough exactly as I am.*

WHO KNEW SO much comfort could come from drawing parakeets—and I've drawn hundreds over the years. All because a total stranger took an hour out of his day, crawled under the table where I was hiding, and gave me a tool that would come to my rescue for years to come, influencing the trajectory of my life forever.

As the only child born to Georgene and Jerry in the

small community of Bountiful, Utah in 1967, my early years should have been a bit more predictable than what they were. More endless summer days running around with the kids in the neighborhood and climbing trees. Less exposure to real-life R-rated scenes in dark apartments. However, my most formidable years of childhood would be stripped away, gone in a blink of an eye.

At eight-years-old, the ground dropped out from under my feet. My environment changed before I had a chance to grasp what was happening. In a flash, I went from routine and a two-parent household to nights left behind, completely alone, the start of darker days to come.

My mom jumped shipped and hopped in a getaway car, choosing Jack as a passenger, a partner who encouraged her to go full speed in a destructive direction because it was the life they both wanted. They pulled me along for the ride seatbelt-free, with the accelerator pedal pushed to the floor.

Please consider with what's to come, this was in an era when seatbelts weren't required or enforced. Seatbelts are a bit of a metaphor here, meaning that we didn't have the extra services, education, and advocates that we have today when it comes to teaching kids about the dangers of addictions, neglect, and sexual advances. Now there are available tools everywhere like hotline numbers, trainings, and Internet sites empowering and encouraging kids to speak up if they are ever put in a dangerous situation. Thank God we have that now, because of those like me who went through hell and decided to talk about it.

Like so many before me, I survived it. There is one reason for that: God. I was guided even when I didn't fully realize it. I had, and still have days, where I want to quit. I don't though, simply out of a belief that I am here for a purpose.

I never felt like I had to conform to the world. I never did drugs, never drank, even when Jack and my mom wanted to include me in their party lifestyle. I wanted to be included in my family—oh, how I wanted to be—but not like that. Not by drinking, partying, or being part of their sick sexual games.

I've always known who I am. The lack of security, safety risks, negligence, and sexual abuse could have torn my will down, but they didn't.

God was there, every step of the way. He delivered one of the clearest messages for my life through a parakeet drawing by a man whose name I'll never know.

But that can come later. For now let's go back to where it all began...

BOUNTIFUL, Utah was a family community and mostly Mormon. Mom was the youngest of five, raised by a loving mother and an abusive, alcoholic father. They called themselves Mormons and tried to fit in, but Grandpa's alcoholic-induced rants kept them from being embraced by their peers. Dad was the second oldest of eight and was raised in a dysfunctional mix of Mormonism and a polygamist cult. By the time they married, Mom and Dad weren't interested in any type of organized religion, or fitting into the young Mormon family neighborhood where they bought their first home.

During the 1960s, it was very rare for women to work in Utah, and as a mom, the expectation was to stay at home. Both of my parents worked, though. My mom never had a desire be traditional.

"She's fun. She's the life of the party." That's how people would describe her, and that was the legacy she clung to.

Being a mother who cooked and cleaned and took care of the house wasn't exactly her type of fun. "Wicked smart and funny" were additional ways others recalled memories of my mom. I would have liked to see that side of her—but what I got was the distant, vapid, and cruel woman. She built a wall up around herself that purposely kept me out, and she never took it down. She had no desire to be a mom —period.

Georgene had dark red hair that was styled in a 1960s updo, held in by endless bobby pins with short, strict bangs that hit just above her perfectly arched eyebrows. She liked to wear all the current styles, and at five-two, it wasn't long before I towered over her, a perfect balance between her height and my dad's six foot, one-inch frame.

Before I was born, she had two miscarriages. She and my dad had been married several years and she was "trying" to be everything that was expected of a young twenty-something woman in the sixties. By the time I came along, she was at the point of accepting her own reality. All she really wanted was someone to hang out with, to party with, and a child who held her back from that was better ignored than embraced.

As a bookkeeper at a local trucking company, Georgene would get home before my dad and by the time he pulled in the driveway, she was ready to go out for the evening. "Jerry, clean up and get dressed, let's go have some fun!" There were always people to see, drinks to drink, cigarettes to smoke.

My dad, a construction worker, put in a lot of hours during the weekdays. Tall and lean, he was a gentle giant with a soothing voice. His work mostly kept him outside during the extremes of Utah's seasons. He would come home, exhausted after a long day of work in the scorching desert sun or cold winter snow, but he continued to work to keep my mom appeased by relenting to her requests. More days than not, he did as she asked and got cleaned up so they could go out on the town.

Once I was born, the responsibility of raising a child began to sway their relationship more toward my dad's preferences. Go to work, come home, and be with family. Simple. My dad loved to come in from work, take his shower, and grab his dinner. He would sit in his recliner with his meal on a TV stand in the living room, while watching the news on our black and white console TV. *Gilligan's Island* was my favorite show, and it came on at the same time as the news. I would get five to ten minutes into the show before Dad would appear and make me switch the dial to the news. Sometimes I would protest and even win, but most times I did not. I would sulk a little bit, but not much because I knew that after dinner, I'd get to crawl in his lap where he'd peel an orange that we would share for dessert.

Dad's family was all nearby. His brothers and sisters lived within fifty miles of Bountiful. One sister lived just down the road from us and his mom lived a few blocks away. My dad was the oldest son. His father died in a ranching accident when he was only nine-years-old. He became "the man of the house" and always felt somewhat responsible for his mom and siblings. He would do anything to help them. They would probably say he was tight with money, but if he could help with a project, lend an ear, or provide advice, he would do it in an instant. He was grounded, generous, and loving.

Although quiet, my dad was also fun. He loved to chase me and once he caught me, he would tickle me until my sides hurt from laughing. Many times, I would be in my room and Dad would sneak in, put his hand over the light switch and quickly turn the lights on and off, calling out, "disco, disco!" I would roll my eyes, laugh, and say, "What do you know about disco, Dad? You only listen to country western music."

I loved the weekends when he wasn't working and would play with me. As an only child, I was mostly used to doing things by myself. I would lose myself for hours perfecting the hair and outfits on my Barbies, scrapping charcoal against my design plates to create templated drawings, and swirling colors and shapes with the Spirographs. I loved art, frequently gravitating to paint-by-numbers and coloring books.

I was a positive, happy child. I had no idea what was headed my way.

But it was coming—fast.

2

DIVORCE

*A*t least most of my first years were spent walking on solid ground. For that, I'm grateful. Despite the contradictions between our family and our Bountiful community, I still considered myself to be raised in a somewhat normal home. Until the day the floor fell.

At eight-years-old, walking the few blocks home from 2nd grade was the highlight of my day. The identical twin boys that lived next door would run up and ask if I wanted to play in their yard when we got home, and I eagerly agreed. We were in the same class, but unable to talk much during school. Our energy was exploding by the end of the day.

With the mountains decorating the backdrop, we left the elementary school behind, flanking the sidewalks to make it out to the main highway that ran through Bountiful. Cars zoomed by, clogging the once-pure air with the heavy scent of gas as we cut through the trailer park. We were laughing, joking, completely carefree, and debating between playing four square or jump rope.

The boys playfully shoved each other, and I happily

clutched my schoolbooks to my chest. No thoughts in our minds, we were content in the present as our immediate goal was to get home. A simple quest.

"Hey, look!" one of the older boys in a group walking ahead of us called out with a whistle. "Let's see what was left behind for us!" With two others, they hurried across the street to the large dumpster that sat behind a long building covered in a black rock facade. The Fifth Amendment, a bar oddly located at the end of our street, a residential neighborhood filled with "good Mormons." At least, that's what I thought we all were. I was beginning to learn the terms "good Mormon," "bad Mormon," and "Jack Mormon," which was the same as a "bad Mormon," but a less polite way of calling them out. I didn't know anyone who was not Mormon, so I suppose at some point I was going to learn how to differentiate who was who. The good Mormons, wholesome, pure, dedicated to the church and its requirements. The others, a small percentage, were considered "bad" or "Jack" Mormons, those that prefer to visit the bars instead of the church.

Utah had strict alcohol laws because of the heavy Mormon population, which encouraged abstaining from drinking. If someone wanted to visit a bar they had to fill out an application and pay an annual fee to become a member, and they had to be a member in order to purchase alcohol in the establishment. Buying an alcoholic drink was then a two-step process. You would buy a mixer, orange juice, tonic water, a soda, and then go to a separate window to buy a mini bottle of alcohol. You could then pour your alcohol into your mixer. Utah might have allowed bars, but they were not going to pour your alcohol and aid in your drinking it. From going into the bar to putting a drink to your lips, they were going to make it as cumbersome as possible! Enough about liquor laws, let's get back to that day...

"Help me up!" Two of the boys stood and lifted the other one into the dumpster. The twins and I stood on the other side of the street, attempting not to be associated with them so we wouldn't get in trouble, but curious as to what they would find.

"Hurry, help me out!" the boy in the dumpster yelled, as the other boys helped him get down safely. They ran back across the street, dodging the cars, excited to show us what treasures they found.

They scored *Playboy* issues and miniature bottles of alcohol that had yet to be completely drained. The older boys shoved the bottles in their pockets and flipped through the magazines on the walk, eventually breaking away from us and taking a different path than where the twins and I were headed.

It became a trend on our walks home. The older boys ran toward the Fifth Amendment to see what the weekly dumpster goods were, perusing the leftovers of sex and alcohol from bar patrons, holding up their treasures and yelling at us to look at what they'd found.

What I didn't realize at the time was how much of a fore-shadowing that was of what was to come in my life. Life's little clues.

One-story ranch homes lined both sides of our long residential street. Twenty houses down, we parted ways. "See you later," the twins called out as they disappeared into their house. I waved and turned into the driveway of my house, planning to go back over to play with them after I dropped my books off.

Before I could get to the front door, it opened and my dad stepped out, hovering on the stoop, alert and fidgety. He usually didn't get home until hours after I arrived from school.

Happily surprised, I ran up to him, "Hi, dad!"

He didn't gloss over the news. "Come in the house. Your mom isn't coming home today."

"Okay." I shuffled past him into the living room. "Does that mean I can sleep with you tonight?" All I knew is that would be a fun surprise if he said yes! None of his other words sank in.

My dad closed the front door and turned to face me. His longer hair and full beard gave him a burly outer appearance that fit into his hunting family, even if he was the one who wouldn't kill a deer. When you looked past those features, you'd see his tender blue eyes that reflected his big heart.

He hesitated, dropped his head a bit and then said, "Sure."

Good, my dad all to myself! I thought as I dropped my books and went to the kitchen for a snack. My dad followed and fixed us turkey sandwiches.

I watched him smooth the mayonnaise on bread with his calloused hands, rough from his day job, gently layering turkey and cheese slices on top. He handed me a plate. I took it to the living room and sat cross-legged on the green shag carpet. He sat in his chair, and we watched TV together. We never had to do much for me to love spending time with him.

At night, I changed into my pajamas and crawled into bed with him, snuggling happily next to his side.

Nights passed without my mom coming home. I didn't mind, but I could tell my dad was bothered by something left unsaid.

"Let's go for a drive," my dad suggested one evening.

We drove, listening to the truck radio as we drove on winding roads up the side of the mountain. The sun lowered in the sky, and my dad's window was down, letting the warm air blow through the window like little kisses on my cheek.

"Rhinestone Cowboy" came on the radio as we turned onto a familiar street. We drove down the paved road, slowly crept by homes, until my dad stopped in front of one of them. He peered out, looking at the driveway and into the well-lit windows of the house.

"What are we doing?" I asked.

"Looking for your mom," my dad responded gently. "That's her friend's house, right there." He pointed at a yellow house with overgrown trees and a lawn that was in need of mowing.

"How will we know if she's here?" I asked while drawing invisible circles on the window with my fingers like binoculars, peering out through them to the house, wondering who was inside.

"She's here," he said. "See, there's her car in the driveway."

"Oh."

Confused, I asked, "Why is she here and not home with us?" I hadn't thought much about her not being home until this moment. Mom rarely played with me anyway, so I didn't feel like I missed much. But why would she choose to stay with her friend and not with us?

My dad stared at the house. "She just needed some time with her friend, that's all. She'll be home soon."

The next evening, Dad said I needed to go back to sleeping in my own bed. I fussed and stomped my feet since I loved the warmth of my dad.

He responded by pulling my favorite bed sheets out of

the dryer and putting them on my bed. "The little sheep are all clean and they miss you."

I relented and slid under the sheets, but something was wrong. I lifted up the top sheet, evaluating both sides of the fabric to investigate. "The sheets aren't right." I lifted the blanket to show him the plain sheet underneath. "The sheep are missing."

"They're not missing," Dad said with a smile. "Look." He pulled the sky blue sheet back and there they were, little white sheep with pink bows on the girls and blue bowties on the boys.

"They're backwards," I said, scrunching my nose. "The sheep go on top of the sheet, not under. That's how Mom puts them on."

"Well, I think this is the way the sheet is supposed to go." He pulled the sheet up and away from me so I could see the characters. "You see? You lie on those sheep there, and then when you pull the top sheet over you, all the little sheep are snuggling with you on both sides. They want to be right next to you."

He kissed my cheek and left the room. I snuggled in and peacefully fell asleep. My dad was right; a sheep sandwich was way better.

It was just us for a week and it was glorious.

Next thing I knew, my mom was back.

She never said where she was or apologized for leaving. A week away, and it was as though nothing strange happened.

Except now my dad was gone for nights at a time.

Slowly, it started to sink in that things would never be the same again. The actual words were never said, but the transferring between houses started.

One day, Mom announced Dad was coming over to pick

me up. "Get your shoes on so you can run out when he gets here."

Run out? Gets here? He's not staying? A simple explanation would have been helpful. Dad pulled up in his green GMC pickup. Mom pushed me out the door. Stumbling forward, I looked back as the storm door slammed shut.

"Come on Gina, I have something to show you!" Dad said through his rolled-down window. I jumped in the passenger seat, and he wrapped me in a big bear hug. I smiled from the comfort of his arms and his presence. Dad and I were back together in his truck as it rolled down the road.

He turned to enter the highway. I didn't get to go on the highway often. Everything we did and everyone we knew were in Bountiful. I looked over at him quizzically but he just gave me a smile.

We weren't on the highway long before taking an exit, making a quick right turn onto a tight frontage road and then a left into a narrow parking lot. A dark brown, two story building stretched from one end of the lot to the other with a flattop roof. A metal stairwell sat at one end, reaching from the ground to the second story walkway. Multiple units lined the bottom and top floors with each apartment divided by their one door and one window.

"What is this?" I asked.

"My new place." Dad pointed to a unit on the second floor about three-quarters of the way down the walkway. "That one is mine."

I pressed my lips together, processing what this meant. Dad had his own place away from our house. He wasn't coming back home.

"Let's go get breakfast!" he suggested. Dad turned the truck around and drove, pulling back onto the highway. A few exits later, he turned into Lee's Café, one of our favorite places to visit. The bubble letters greeted us, promising a delicious meal. We slid into a booth and ordered. The waitress knew what my dad wanted. Everyone who knew my dad could predict his order. Pancakes. The only question was how he would have his pancakes this time. Would it be an egg in between two buttermilk cakes, a tall stack with flavored syrup, maybe peanut butter and jelly spread generously over the top? I colored on my kids' paper menu, stealing glances at him while he considered his options. The moment dad said, "pancakes," the twinkle returned in his eyes. It may be the one thing he loved more than me!

Afterward, he took me to explore one of his newest job sites. Next, we bowled, and had a great time. Then he dropped me back off at my mom's house. No longer his house; only hers.

Still confused, I entered through the side door of the carport, passing through the mudroom and into the kitchen, surprised to see the kitchen table covered with bags of groceries.

My mom didn't pay attention as I walked past her. Gabbing away into the faded yellow phone in her hand, the cord stretched and curled with her every move as she peeked into the bags. Talking to the person on the other end, she said, "Yeah, the church just dropped off food."

We were not churchgoers, but the Mormon Church was taking care of her—taking care of us. I wondered who had called them. *Why did they bring food? Dad would have brought us food if we needed it. Why didn't she just tell him we needed groceries?* My eight-year-old mind couldn't put together the puzzle pieces fast enough.

Other people in the community had it figured out, though.

I went across the street to play with my friend Mary. Knocking on the door, I saw her head peek out from the window curtains. She opened the front door, just enough for me to see her face, and whispered, "I can't play with you anymore."

"Why not?" I asked, replaying the school week in my mind, wondering what I did wrong to her.

"My parents said I can't play with you anymore," Mary repeated.

"Why not?" I pressed, equally confused and sad that she couldn't be my friend anymore.

"Because *your* parents," she lowered her voice even more, "are getting divorced."

Everyone else knew before I fully realized it: everything in my life was changing.

Everything in my life was changing. I felt out of place. Where exactly did I belong these days? We lived almost every way the Mormon Church said not to, and the church was all around us. At eight-years-old, I had no say in it, yet I was continually affected by the decisions the adults in my life made.

My dad had been my saving grace. He could talk me through any problem. To this one, he would have said something like, "Every family is a little different, they believe in different things. It's okay and you know I love you, right?" He was my protector in the house, until I was reduced to seeing him only one brief day per week. The court systems back then assumed the mother was the safest place for the child. They didn't know my mom, though.

Despite being lawfully responsible to watch me six days of the week, it wasn't long before my mom retreated into the comfort of the lifestyle that always suited her best. Alcohol, drugs, parties, and men—the fun that motherhood couldn't provide.

Having a daughter to take care of wasn't a factor to be considered. If anything, I was a burden to the life she wanted.

So, she invited someone else who could deliver the fun she craved.

Jack.

3

JACK

I remember the first day I met him.

A knock on the door, and my mom answered it. I looked up as a man stepped inside the house. He looked too comfortable, as though he'd been to our house before, despite this being the first time I'd seen him.

Who is this? I wondered but I didn't ask out loud.

"Get up!" my mom directed me. "Come say hi."

I left my crayons on the floor and followed her to the door. Using her legs as a shield, I peeked around to glance at him.

"This is Jack." My mom introduced him as she pulled me from behind her legs to stand before the man with nothing blocking my way. Leathery, tanned skin, thinning blond-gray hair, and turquoise eyes that shined, reflecting off his sky blue, snap-buttoned shirt. "He drives a semi-truck," she explained. She must have met him at work.

My dad just left, and now there was a new man standing in our house. Jack couldn't have been any more opposite of my dad. Eighteen years older, six inches shorter, a swollen nose with big pores. He reminded me of a bulldog, except not the cute kind. Jack smiled, reaching out his hand past his hard potbelly to pat my head.

He walked around us, crossed the room, and grabbed a chair from the kitchen table. He brought it into the living room and sat down. That's where he was the rest of the night as he smoked cigarettes with my mom.

I analyzed his casual nature and wondered what his relationship was with her. Once he started asking me questions about what I liked to do, I no longer cared. I ate up the attention. I liked having someone talk to me and ask me questions about what I enjoyed doing. He wanted to see what I was coloring and asked the names of my stuffed animals.

Within weeks, Jack had moved in and that same kitchen chair stayed in the living room, sitting right next to Dad's recliner. Everyone kept changing my world, and no one asked how I felt about it.

Jack fell into a pattern. We all did. It became normal to wake up and see him sitting in his chair watching TV or in the kitchen cooking something for breakfast. Sometimes, he wasn't there. "He's on the road," Mom said, explaining he picked up loads and drove them across the country, gave them to someone else, then picked up another load to bring back to Utah. He'd be gone for a week or longer at times.

I tried not to look forward to Jack coming back when he was gone on his long hauls, but I did. He gave me more attention than my mom ever had.

"Did you get your homework done?" he asked in the evenings.

"Yes."

"What did you work on today?"

I told him about the newest lesson and filled him in on the stories from school.

I enjoyed talking to Jack. Mom didn't seem to care much about what I did, ignoring me. On the other hand, Jack appeared interested in how I was spending my time each day and what I was learning in school. He brought excitement into the house.

I studied my mom's changing demeanor from when she was alone with me versus when Jack was around. He would walk through the door and her eyes would brighten. She still wouldn't say much, but she'd cackle her smoker's laugh, affirming everything Jack said was hilarious. They would sit and watch TV together for all hours of the night.

Jack's presence in the household brought me into the loop. He extended the gift of parenting that my mom couldn't offer. Sometimes I'd sit in Dad's recliner, on the other side of Jack, feeling like maybe I could belong. Mom always tried to exile me, even when it was just she and I living together.

One night, Jack suggested, "Let's make dinner."

"Okay!" I jumped off the recliner, ready to help.

Jack immediately reached for the cold hotdogs from the fridge. I sighed, disappointed that it was hotdogs again.

Hotdogs were a staple. Mom would cook them the same way each time. Boil them in a pan, then lay them on a baking sheet, splitting them open lengthwise and layering on a mountain of instant mashed potatoes. I'd watch closely as she shredded cheddar cheese and let it sprinkle from her fingertips onto the mashed potatoes. She loved cheddar cheese. She would cut off a chunk of the golden block to munch on while she slid the baking pan under the broiler. After a few minutes, the bronzed, gooey dish was ready to eat.

Jack had a different twist on hotdogs. I was in awe as he pulled both ground hamburger *and the hotdogs* out of the fridge, so I climbed onto the counter and watched carefully. After turning on the stove, he minced the hamburger into fine little pieces. Handing me the spatula, he said, "Go ahead and stir carefully while I chop onions." Once he threw most of the diced pieces in, the fragrance rose from the browning meat and filled the kitchen. My stomach growled. Jack added tomato sauce and mustard to top it off, stirring them together so the colors swirled in the skillet like art before merging together.

As the ingredients simmered, the wonderful scent grew so strong it competed with the stale cigarette smoke, a welcomed change. Jack grabbed a head of broccoli from the fridge and showed me how to wash it.

"When I was your age, I was cooking for myself." His bushy eyebrows furrowed in concentration while skillfully cutting the vegetable. "If you wanted to eat, you pulled the vegetables from the ground and cooked them yourself."

Jack set up the metal steamer on the stove, dropping the veggies in and covering them so they could cook peacefully.

He moved around like a master of the kitchen, and I watched his ease with fascination. Dad never really cooked. Mom would make sandwiches and her hotdog dish. The only time we had elaborate meals like what Jack was cooking was when we visited my aunts or grandparents.

"If you want something made right, you do it yourself," he continued to preach. "Grab those plates."

I reached for three plates and set them on the counter. Jack scooped the vegetables out and placed one hotdog in a bun on each plate, smothering them in the special hamburger sauce and the leftover diced raw onion.

It was the most delicious meal I had eaten in our house. I was filled with pride, savoring each bite I took.

When Jack's friends were at the house, they would

request, "Hey, make those special dogs and sauce for us!" He had a meal, created by him, that people loved. He was the closest thing to a chef I had ever met, and I loved it.

He was the first one to teach me how to cook and also, about saving.

Jack had a Folgers coffee can hidden in the cupboard above the stove. He would pull it out sometimes and set it on the dining room table. Reaching deep into his pockets, he emptied them of coins, throwing each one into the can.

"It's important to save money, Gina," he told me as I watched.

"How much is in there?" I asked, peering into the copper mixture.

Jack shrugged with a grin on his face. "That's the fun. It's as good of a time as any to count it." Jack dumped out the contents, the dings of the coins hitting the table like a slot machine. A well-organized roll of bills held tightly together by rubber bands bounced off the table and rolled across the floor. Giggling, I ran after it and handed it back to him.

Shoving coins aside, he organized them into groups. Counting them, pushing them into coin wrappers, closing off each one by folding the edges. "See? Quarters just turned into ten dollars. These nickels are now two dollars. These dimes are five dollars." It was like magic.

I listened to him rattle off the numbers with satisfaction, and jot down the final count on a piece of paper with the date.

"That's how you save money," he said as he put the full container back into the cupboard. "Nice and safe so the banks can't take it."

No one had talked to me about money, outside of lessons we learned in school. I was intrigued by how quickly a little coin could multiply and add value. Coins turned into dollars right in front of me. Every little one added up to big value. It was a lesson that stuck with me.

Jack believed in saving, but also enjoyed buying things.

A trip to Kmart typically meant I got to go into the Folgers can for two or three dollars to pick something out at the store. I never got an allowance, so it was the only time I had money of my own to spend. I liked going to Kmart for that sole reason. Okay, and for the blue light special. I never seemed to have enough money for the blue light special, but I ran over to see what it would be nonetheless. Jack would never run with me. He never seemed impressed enough to rush for much.

Jack's biggest obsession was with cars. He had subscriptions to all the car magazines. Sitting at the kitchen table in the evenings, he would flip through them while tapping his cigarette against the amber ashtray as it caught the ashes. Corvettes were his favorite. Anytime he saw somebody with one, he'd stop and talk to the owners. Corvette owners loved talking about their cars just as much. I wondered if he was saving up for one.

I cautiously admired the way Jack chatted with people. From afar, he appeared confident and cool, at ease with the world around him. My dad was quiet, more introverted. It was another stark difference between the two. In the beginning, I liked watching Jack talk to everyone around him. As long as I was at a distance, I couldn't hear his words. It was better that way.

We didn't live in my mom and dad's Bountiful home for long. Summer came and we moved. The end of the third grade school year brought the beginning of the end of my childhood.

We moved to an apartment in King's Row Manor, far away from the safety that I once knew. No longer in a quiet neighborhood. We were now in the middle of a bustling city, in a huge apartment complex. It was loud, fast moving, and a shock to my system. Especially as everything became Jack's world.

I worried about my dad. Would he know where to find me? He did! He picked me up every Sunday, just like he always had. He asked how I liked the new apartment and even though I didn't like it, I tried to sound happy about it. After all, he was living in an apartment now too.

We settled into a new routine. Well, Mom and Jack did. In the mornings, they turned the TV on with the sound up loud. Were they competing with the neighbor's music that blared through the walls? Or maybe the sound of the baby crying in the apartment under us? They watched the news and game shows like *The Price is Right*, shouting out their answers while the coffee pot hissed out black coffee. Once it was empty, their cups were refilled with Black Velvet Whiskey, regardless of the time of the morning.

I hated the smell of Black Velvet. I still do.

When Jack went on the road, sometimes my mom went, sometimes she stayed behind.

She despised staying behind.

Mom would walk Jack to the door, kiss him goodbye, and watch as he pulled out from the driveway. I stood in the living room witnessing the anger light like a match just after being struck across the side of the box. Her anger flickered then burst into a flame.

She shut the door, stormed past me, ensuring that no part of her body touched mine. Heaven forbid a mother touch her daughter.

She was salty because she was forced to stay behind. Maybe because of me, maybe because of work. I wasn't sure.

But it felt like my fault.

She didn't want to be with me.

So I would grab a coloring book and crayons, returning to my room to draw a brighter world than the one I found myself in.

On the nights Jack was gone, I would crawl into bed with my mom at her surprising request. She liked having me sleep with her when Jack wasn't there. These were the only times she softened. Maybe she was scared to be home alone at night. I didn't know, but anytime I got to sleep next to someone else, I took it. The fact that she would talk softly to me, often doing relaxation exercises was a bonus. "Flex your right foot, then relax it," she coached.

"What does flex mean?" I asked.

"Tighten it up, squeeze the muscle tight as you can. That's flexing."

"Oh." I practiced it, squeezing muscles I didn't know I could control, wanting to impress her.

"Do you have it now? Can you do it?" she asked, genuinely interested in my success to do this.

"Yes…yes, I got it."

"Okay, now flex your calf muscle, tight as you can, then release it and feel it relax."

"I'm doing it!" I exclaimed, more from thrill that she was doing something with me than the fact that I figured out flexing.

"Okay, let's keep going." She continued to tell me where on my body I should tighten and relax.

"Now, flex your butt."

I stopped and stared at her. "Flex my butt?"

Her smoker's cackle started low in her chest and rose into a jagged giggle before converting into a full-fledged laugh. I joined her, holding my side from laughing so hard.

It was one of the only times I remember laughing with her.

One night, as I crawled into her and Jack's king-sized bed, Mom turned on the made-for-TV movie *The Stepford Wives*. Nightly commercials for weeks had set her anticipation high. She was *not* going to miss it.

The ashtray sat between us, as she tapped her cigarette into it while sipping on Black Velvet and Coke. While she was propped up on a pillow watching the movie, I pretended to be asleep. I opened one eye, lifting my head to see over the roundness of her hip, peeking at the TV. Robotic women, perfect homemakers, and obedient wives moved about in low cut pastel dresses on the screen. The non-robotic women were angry. Their friends were acting strange. Husbands were nervous and evasive. The angry women scurried about trying to figure out what was going on, until they too became perfect little robots.

It was intriguing and terrifying. I watched with a new awareness wondering how many robots were around me.

Suddenly, Mom got out of bed, walked over to the TV and turned the volume up. I shut my eyes tightly so she wouldn't know I had been watching. I stayed that way until she got back into bed, turned her back to me and lit another cigarette. It took me some time to relax enough, yet somehow, I managed to fall asleep.

"Gina, get out of bed!" Mom said while shaking my arm.

"What?" I asked, rubbing my eyes open.

"You're talking in your sleep. Go to your room," she demanded. "You're too loud!"

I looked at the TV that was still on, wondering how it was possible I was louder than that.

I grabbed my teddy bear and went back to my room, sleeping alone in my bed once again. That night I dreamt about men in the town who turned the women into robots. Their expectations of obedience and perfectionism loomed over me, and for weeks after I wondered if everyone were a robot, eyeing Mom and Jack and their calloused nature especially.

4

THE PARAKEETS

*M*om and Jack began bringing gifts for me when they went shopping or returned from trips on the truck. Usually it was a magnet. Sometimes it was a t-shirt. Once it was an ashtray. An ashtray for a nine-year-old is odd, right? Trust me when I say the whole thing was odd! They had stopped interacting with me much, yet they brought me gifts and expected me to be VERY excited about them. I normally was more confused than excited.

But one time, they brought something big. So big that Jack was struggling to walk up the stairs to the apartment with the awkward size of it.

A cage. Definitely a cage. Now what's inside?

I squealed when they lifted the sheet.

Two beautiful little parakeets perched inside. One was a peaceful green, the color of the grass on a spring day, with a yellow head. The other was sky blue with gray feathers and a white head. Both had blue feathers in their tails.

"What are their names?" I asked, sticking my fingers in the cages, trying to pet them.

"You get to name them," Jack said.

"I do?" It seemed like an immense responsibility, and I was surprised they gave it to me. For some reason, I knew right away the blue one was Pat. The green one I wasn't as sure. It took a few hours before a name felt right. Jack and Mom were already saddled up on the couch with drinks and cigarettes in their hands when I made the announcement.

"This one," I said excitedly pointing to the green one, "is Nino."

"That's a funny name. Why Nino?" Jack inquired.

I shrugged as I wiggled the tip of my finger through the slender bar cages. "Hi, Nino," I cooed, already in love. I had no idea where the name came from, but I knew that was perfect for him. However, my mom tried to discourage me from choosing it.

"You can't name one of them a boring, plain name like Pat and the other one a crazy name no one has ever heard of."

"Why not?" I asked confused. I didn't know there were bird naming rules.

"Because you can't! It's that simple. Pick another name."

"Okay," I said, defeated, hating her verbal attacks. "I'll think of something else." But I couldn't. Nothing else came to me. No other name was as fitting.

The tug-of-war continued for days. "Did you pick another name?" my mom would ask.

"No."

"Pick another name!" She yelled as though the fate of the world depended on it.

"I can't think of another name! He looks like a Nino to me. I'm trying!" Tears threatened my eyes. They said I could name the birds. I did, and she hated it.

"Don't you yell at me!"

Jack stood up and came to her rescue, ready to defend as

though he was a drunken knight. "Who do you think you are, yelling at your mom?"

"I didn't mean to yell," I quickly apologized and tried to explain, "She yelled at me. She keeps getting on me, telling me to pick another name, but I can't. I'm trying!"

"Go to your room!" he shouted back.

I escaped down the hall to my room, glanced at Nino before I left and whispered a plea of protection. Mom and Jack were super mad. Would they take the parakeets back? I was already attached.

In time, Mom finally stopped asking me to change Nino's name. She stopped talking about it all together. I never said anything either. I just called him Nino. Nino, Nino, Nino. *My* Nino.

I could watch the little parakeets squawk and dance around in their cages all day. Sometimes they would stop and preen each other. Other times they'd bob their heads and sing to each other. I just wished I could play with them. I really wished I could play with them! All I could do was stick my finger in the cages.

I felt so grown-up taking care of them. Covering them with their blanket each night and whispering goodnight. It was just like when my dad used to pull my covers up around my neck, kissing my forehead with a whispered, "sweet dreams." Now I got to be the adult, tucking the birds in each night.

Every morning, I woke up excited to be with them again. I raised the covering on the cage and greeted them. "Good morning!" Their sweet little spirits squawked in return. When I gave them food and fresh water, they did a happy dance, my favorite part of the day.

Sometimes thick, blue tail feathers would fall from them into the bottom of the cage. Other times, from their little face feathers, the ones with a dot would appear. Those were my favorites!

I looked around to make sure Jack didn't see me, and took the feathers out from the bottom of the cage. I hid them in a velvet jewelry box that I kept safe in my room.

Jack didn't like it because he said that the feathers carried germs. That meant nothing to me. I loved every part of those birds.

The brass cage sat tall and regal next to our overstuffed orange couch. An ornate gold mirror with two tall candlestick holders, one mounted on each side of the mirror hung over the couch. My mom walked right past the parakeets several times a day as she made her way to her spot on the couch. She'd sit there, like a permanent stain on the cushion, smoking one cigarette after another, not looking at or engaging with the birds at all. Just like me.

Pat only lived for three months. I lifted the sheet up one morning and there he was, lying peacefully on the bottom of the cage. I wondered if he couldn't handle the continual inhalation of smoke from my mom. I couldn't blame him.

The stale smoke mixed with the dirty parakeet cage was potent, especially noticeable after walking in from outside. Not that the air was much better out there. Surrounded by gas stations, convenience stores and a main highway that separated our apartment building with a truck stop, I suppose they were both potent smells, just in very different ways.

I hated cleaning the birdcage. Jack would help me each time, but he didn't like cleaning it either. He wasn't as nice to me when that chore came about.

Sometimes we would let Nino fly around the apartment while cleaning the cage. Nino enjoyed dodging around, looking for a place to land and catch his breath. I watched him in awe as he flew freely around the room. How good that must have felt to him, flapping his wings, free to roam from here to there. Nino discovered that perching on top of the curtain rungs above the window was a safe place to rest out of reach. Jack was so short that he couldn't reach him. "You goddamn bird. Get your ass down here now!" he would yell at this tiny parakeet. Nino would cock his head and look down at Jack, knowing he had all the time in the world to relax on his perch. I stifled a laugh.

"I'll squeeze the life out of your fucking bird if you laugh again," Jack threatened. When he got mean, it was scary.

Jack didn't like what he couldn't control.

When days became darker, I would spend many hours lying on the carpet next to the cage, crying. Nino would rub his beak on the sandpaper perch covers, chirping and singing to brighten my day.

He was my companion when I had no one else. He was the bright light I needed in the house. He bobbed his head and danced around on the days I felt the most afraid. I wondered how Nino could be so happy. Did he not feel the same fear I did? Or did he, and he chose to dance instead?

5
_____

JACK'S TRUE COLORS

*J*ack taught me to cook and save money. He also was the one who disciplined me. My mom, on the other hand, was an equal opportunity avoider. She avoided me period. So when I pushed buttons, Jack would set me back in line.

Sometimes I respected that. There were times when even I knew I deserved getting in trouble.

The problem with Jack was that it was hard to determine if I did something wrong, or if he was just in a bad mood, ready to lash out at anyone who crossed his path. Another side of him was beginning to emerge. I didn't know what it was, but I could feel the air change, and I didn't like it one bit.

Jack didn't take crap from anyone. Originally from Detroit, he acted tough and hard, and I knew he had had his own ass beat at some point. Always passive-aggressive, at least he knew when to fight and when to walk away. Sneering and mumbling under his breath, sly with how loud he was and whom he targeted to degrade—dependent on how many drinks he had in him. There was always a reason why someone else was at fault, and it was always shaped by Jack's biases.

My mom willingly submitted as his puppet, which fed into his control tendencies.

Jack would shove a few dollars in my hand. "Get out of the house. Go pick something out across the street. Don't come back for an hour."

My mom disappeared into their bedroom, and I got the hint. I took his money, happy to have a chance to be out of the house.

At ten-years-old, I stood on the sidewalk of the busy four-lane highway, waiting for the cars to slow down long enough so I could cross the street and get to the nearest drugstore. There weren't any crosswalks, so I had to make-do. Once it was clear, I ran as fast as I could across two lanes, the adrenaline pushing me across to the center median in record time. I paused and waited for the next two lanes to be clear and off I ran again.

What parent in their right mind would send a kid across a busy four-lane highway without a crosswalk?

Oh yeah, my mom and Jack.

Opening the door to the drugstore, I browsed the aisles, searching for something fun to do.

Puzzles. Cards for solitaire. Coloring books. Fashion plates. All things I was used to buying to keep myself entertained. I never looked at the things that required more than one person to play. After moving away from the twins and Mary ending our friendship, I had no more friends to play with.

I settled on a latch hook rug project. I held the kit in my hands, trying to figure out if it came with a latch hook or not. It didn't say anything, and I didn't have one at home. Jack didn't give me enough money to get both. So I reached for an individual latch hook, ripped a little hole in the packaging of the kit, and shoved the hook inside. I went to the register and paid. As I walked out the door, a security guard stopped me. He had witnessed every move I made.

The guard took me in the back office and called Mom. I sat there, unfeeling, just watching the events unfold. I didn't think it was a big deal. A kit didn't have a hook that was necessary for completion of the product, so I added what the kit needed so I could create the rug. Simple.

It was only when Mom showed up to get me that I wondered if I did something wrong. I would have to know what was right and wrong to be able to comprehend that, which was nothing she took responsibility to show me in ten years of life.

She stormed out of the office, and I followed her. We got in her car and rode back home in silence.

When we arrived, Jack seized my arm with one hand while he pulled the belt from his pants with his other hand. I resisted his grip and tried to squirm away.

"Georgene, hold your goddamn thief down!"

Mom held my legs, one of the few touches I received from her, while Jack repeatedly whipped my butt with a belt.

It was the first time he hit me, and I was shocked.

And I was pissed at my mom for helping him. It wouldn't be the last time.

When it was over, I lay on the carpet next to Nino's cage, as hot tears streaked down my face. He chirped and sang, and I was grateful that at least he understood. I wasn't a thief. I was a good person. I just didn't know I was making a bad decision.

Jack's interest in my days started taking a shadowy turn. I used to love his questions and his attention, but even so young, I could feel the level of discomfort he brought every time he opened his mouth.

"What's your teacher's name again?" Jack asked.

My guard immediately shot up, but in an effort to tell him about my day, I said, "Her name is Ms. Randall. She was in a good mood today and told a funny story. She said—"

Jack cut me off with a snort. "A good mood, huh? She must have gotten banged last night."

I tried to ignore his comment and the visual it created in my mind. I didn't understand completely what "being banged" meant, but Jack was dark. It was best that I didn't completely get it. I continued, "Ms. Johnson let us draw for an extra twenty minutes today."

Jack didn't care about the drawing. "Does Ms. Johnson wear tight shirts? How far down are they buttoned? Can you see her tits?"

I swallowed my frustration. "We also had a new kid join our class today."

"What's his name?"

I perked up, relieved that he had a real question for once. "It's a girl. Her name is Talia."

"Talia? What color is she?"

"Um, Brown?"

Jack snorted again and muttered under his breath something I was glad I couldn't hear.

I had a good day at school. I wanted to tell someone about it. *It was a good day.* I was happy. I worked hard to stay focused on that. Jack tried to make my stories and my days ugly and dirty, but I was learning not to grant him the ability to do that.

Taking a deep breath, I tried again. "And um, the teacher showed her—"

Jack cut me off, whipping around to point a finger in my face and jeered, "And um, you're dumb."

What? I stood still, wondering if I should finish my story. I continued on until I ran into an "um" again.

"And um, you're dumb!" Jack mocked me again, more forcefully this time.

I didn't feel stupid until he said it twice. My face reddened, and I stopped talking about my day.

It wasn't the last time I heard his infamous retort, one that only he found clever.

I didn't want to be dumb. I stopped saying "um," and made sure to speak eloquently, especially when he was around. To this day, I have Jack to thank for my public speaking skills. No joke – it's been a constant compliment from others throughout my life. All due to the drive to not "be dumb."

Jack had an opinion about everything, and he never held that opinion back.

At such a young age and without the access to TV, music, movies, and Internet that kids have today, I didn't grasp some things he said. But the delivery and combination of words shook my system, and that was enough to know they weren't said with love.

He was naturally gruff, but I didn't fear him most of the time. Maybe I should have. Jack's choice of swear words and inappropriate terms dotted his conversational tones. It was only when he would turn especially angry when I became scared.

When Jack would say, "Let's go. We need groceries," I tried not to groan.

My mom grabbed her purse and headed toward the front door, obedient. I, on the other hand, was not.

"I don't want to go." I knew what this trip would bring:

embarrassment, shame, the desire to hide under a rock. It wasn't fun to go out in public with them these days.

"Get in the goddamn car," Jack demanded, gruffer yet. That was the end of any argument.

I hated it. Windows up, capturing the toxicity of their lit cigarettes in a suffocating vapor around us, The Eagles singing "Take it to the Limit" on the radio. Jack yelled over the music, pointing out the year of every car he saw and ensuring mom and I knew which ones were pieces of shit.

As soon as we arrived at the store, Jack slid out of his seat, loudly slamming the car door to announce his arrival, and squared his shoulders. Raising his head to appear taller, he swaggered into the store, oblivious if we were following him.

"Let's go, wop! Stop dragging your feet," Jack said turning to look at me.

I had no clue what a wop was and knew it was probably better not to know.

My mom's bare chest under her tight t-shirts also made me feel uncomfortable, especially as the chill of the grocery store revealed more of her. "No bra when we go out," Jack told her more than once. When he said, "let's go to the store," she stopped in her tracks, reached behind her back and deftly undid the hooks, sliding her bra out of her sleeve like a pro. Anything to make him happy.

A robot.

I don't know why he cared. He barely looked at her in the grocery store. Instead, he walked up to another woman gripping a cart.

Jack pointed to this woman's chest with his tongue almost hanging out of his mouth. "Those gotta be double Ds. If you don't have anyone to lick those, I can give you my number."

This was the reason I hated going out with them these days. His actions were consistent. It was always a guess as to who might engage with him and who wouldn't. This one did, flattered that Jack got her bra size right, not caring about the other woman and child tagging along.

I turned to my mom, waiting for a sign that she registered what Jack was doing—I looked for hurt, anger, any emotion at all. Maybe she would pull him away so we could get out of here quicker and not make a scene. If I could hear his degrading words, I knew she could. But her face remained impassive as she picked through the apples. She was a zombie following him around. She was a Stepford Wife.

I followed her lead and busied myself with the apples, acknowledging the beautiful ones and the bruised ones.

In Bountiful, I had played with the kids I grew up with, like Mary and the twins next door.

When we moved to King's Row, the families were different. Sometimes I saw kids playing on a big grassy area, but I didn't know which apartments they lived in. There were hundreds of apartments. Tiny little homes all stuck next to and on top of each other. When the kids were done playing, they ran in all different directions, like a cue ball hitting a newly racked set of pool balls. They were not nice kids either. They were little gangs of nine- and ten-year-olds. I would wave from across the lawn, but they would just turn away.

"Who's the new girl? She probably won't live here long. Don't talk to her."

As I was getting ready to wave and say "hi" to a girl a few

years older than me, she yelled out, "Take a picture, brat! It'll last longer!"

I missed my friends in Bountiful desperately.

Then Sarah came along. Finally a new friend I liked who gave me a chance. Sarah was nice, and she liked playing Barbies.

Since I had just gotten a new Barbie, I asked her if she wanted to come over to play. I was ecstatic when she said yes.

We went in my room, closed the door and played dress up with Barbies as I showed her all the different outfits I loved to make. She enjoyed crafting imaginary relationships between the dolls and would use different voices to represent each one. She pretended the Barbies were off to ride in the Barbie convertible on a fun day exploring the city, doing all the fun things normal people did. I just cared about doing their hair and dressing them in fun clothes. I didn't have as much of an imagination as she did.

I forgot what it was like to play with someone else, how enjoyable it could be and loved having her over.

Then we made the mistake of driving the convertible down the hallway and into the living room to play.

Jack was sitting in his chair, smoking and looking through his magazine, "What are you girls doing?"

"Playing Barbies," I answered, nodding to the dolls on the floor that we brought out with us.

Jack held up the magazine in his hand. A naked girl posed on the front, her body fully exposed except for the words on the front and the angle at which she stood. *Playboy*. I had seen this magazine too many times. From the older boys who would pull them out of dumpsters to the ones Jack stored here in the house, typically covered by his car magazines.

"This is what little girls grow up to be," he said while flipping through the pages, displaying the naked women in seductive poses. "This is what you girls will be." His icy blue eyes sparkled as a smile spread across his face. He wasn't teasing us; he wasn't even trying to scare us. In his mind he was giving us information that we needed to know. And he liked it.

Stunned, my stomach flipped and knotted. I knew he looked at those magazines, and his view on women in general was starting to click in my young mind. Jack's crude comments were old news, but I couldn't believe he was saying that to my friend, another nine-year-old that he had never met before.

Mom sat on the couch, smoking a cigarette. I looked to her for guidance, but she kept her eyes on the television. She didn't stand up to Jack, didn't protect us, didn't make sure we didn't believe being a *Playboy* centerfold was all we, as young girls, should aspire to be.

Sarah jumped up and ran out the front door. Not surprisingly, her parents didn't let her come back over.

Devastated, that was the last time I invited a friend over to play. It was no longer safe for me to even consider having friends.

I was grateful to at least have a bedroom I could disappear into. I was there a lot to escape the world I now lived in. As an only child, I had no one to confide in, no one to compare what was "normal" and what was not. No one to share my thoughts with. No one to confirm that this new world was getting scary. I spent most of my time alone. I didn't know anything different. It started shifting from normal to a necessity, though. My room was one of the only remaining places I felt safe.

6

THE POOL

There were not many things I liked about the King's Row Apartments, but one cool part was the outdoor pool. Surrounded by a metal gate, the residents would lounge in white chairs around the rectangular pool while kids splashed and played. The sunlight was a welcomed contrast to our dark apartment and the stale smells.

The complex's Laundromat was in a small hideaway off the side of the pool, so we would deposit our clothes in the washer before heading to the pool. I loved pushing the quarters through the slot of the washing machines, waiting for them to clink so we could power them up, just to watch the clothes slosh around and around. Jack made me rush to the Laundromat to stake a claim on the machines before anyone could use them, long before Jack and Mom were even ready to go. They were busy packing the cooler full of drinks for the pool. In the meantime, I had to throw a shirt in the washer so no one would take "his" machine. I sat next to it, terrified that another adult would yell at me for it, like a law was broken. One *was* broken, in the sense of communal respect.

Many times, we went back to the Laundromat after swimming to find our clothes moved out of the machines and onto the table by others who needed to wash their clothes. We would be gone for hours between loads, sometimes not returning to the laundry room until the next day. Jack and Mom didn't view it as anything they did wrong, though. Instead, it was disrespectful for other people to touch our clothes. *How dare they!* I can still hear Jack screaming as he flipped out when he noticed his pants were gone, stolen from the pile of clothes on the table.

They made the laundry room and pool miserable areas to be.

Soaking up the sun by the pool should have been a perfect way to burn time during the summers. It started off fun, but soon, like most things with Jack, the fun only went so far before it turned embarrassing. Dread would teeter on the edge of a good time as I waited for the trigger that would ruin the fun.

Jack and Mom always claimed two lounge chairs by throwing their items on it. I ran to the other side of the pool as far away as I could get. I didn't want anyone to know I was with them. I jumped into the warm water, waiting for my body to adjust to the initial shock.

From my safe distance in the pool, I kept one eye on Jack and Mom as they said hi to the people sitting next to them. Laughing and waving as though they were the guests of honor at a party and everyone was waiting for them to arrive.

I knew a ticking time bomb hid under the surface of it all, counting down to the explosion. Jack would eventually piss someone off, sputtering curses for everyone to hear as though he was the only one entitled to take up space. It was sickly predictable. The only question was when it would happen and which poor soul would be at the brunt of it.

In the apartment, Jack and Mom rarely moved from their chosen spots, cigarettes dangling from their mouths and drink after drink in their hands with limited liveliness. This, their gregarious persona at the pool, didn't feel real. None of this. I formed a circle with my hand and put it in front of my eye as though it was the lens of a video camera. This wasn't my life. This was someone else's story. A show. A movie. Fake. Mentally, I disassociated.

Mom removed her black cover-up, showing off her low-cut bikini top, exposing the full size of her enormous breasts. Jack whistled loudly. "Those are my titties!" he announced loud enough for everyone to hear as he grabbed at the air with pinchers. Mom laughed and shook her head, her red bangs flapping in her face. They didn't see the shock followed by disgust in the faces of people around them. I did. I noticed it all. The fake video camera kept rolling. Embarrassed, I ducked into the pool and swam as if I was an Olympic champion, training alone and on a mission to win a medal.

Jack cracked open his cooler and took out his thermos, pouring Black Velvet into a plastic cup, filling it the rest of the way with Coke while he struck up a conversation with a couple of other men sitting by. I watched one drink after another go to his lips as the volume of his voice would carry poolside. It mixed in with another man's voice who was equally as perverted as Jack. What started as a request for a light for his cigarette turned into a competition for the Most Crass Award. Jack found a match.

My mom sat at the edge of the pool, swinging her legs in the water. An audience of young boys gathered around her.

As she leaned over to talk and laugh with them, one of her breasts slipped from the thin fabric containing them. Jack saw the reveal and pointed it out to his buddies. He whistled again with a grin, proud of what his woman could show the world. The young boys bobbed in the water with big grins on their faces, whispering to one other. My mom had no idea she had fallen out of her swimsuit. She was already too drunk to realize it, simply eating up any attention she received. I put my hands over my face, mortified. I hoped no one knew I was with them. *It's just a movie. I'm watching a movie. I'm not associated with this.* The other kids treated me as an outcast as it was. I didn't want any more problems, especially at the pool. The pool was supposed to be a fun escape!

"Hey you!" Jack yelled. Although he always abrupt and loud, his tone took on a certain bitter edge when he was angry. This was it. "Those are my pants! You stole my fucking pants!"

He stood up from his chair and chased a man out of the pool gate and down the sidewalk. I ducked under the water, afraid about what would happen next.

When I came up for air, Jack had returned, cursing like a frantic tornado.

"Hey, there are kids here. Watch your language," another man chastised him.

Jack's cheeks, already heated from the sudden bout of exercise, managed to turn even redder. He wiggled a finger in the guy's face. "Shut the fuck up! Don't you fucking tell me how to talk. This pool is mine. I pay to use this."

He downed his drink and gathered up the pool bag and our things. My mom pulled herself away from her tiny admirers, tucking her breast back into her swimming suit, stoic and drunk, not caring about the scene. "Fuck off. All of you. Fuck off!" Jack continued to yell as he walked out, taking my towel with him.

I slipped out of the pool, shivering as I followed them from a distance, wet and dripping, but also from mortification.

It was a few weeks before we returned to the pool again. Jack made it clear that he had better not see anyone with his clothes on again, mumbling under his breath as we entered through the pool gate. Once we crossed the threshold into the pool area his focus shot straight forward, his shoulders squared, his hard potbelly leading the way as he claimed his spot. I was relieved to see there were only a dad and his son at the pool today. They left soon after we arrived, and I wondered if he had had a run-in with Jack at some point in the past. Jack's reputation preceded him.

After a few hours, we returned from the pool, tapped out from the sun. My pale skin reflected the scorch of the sun. I said hi to Nino and gave him fresh water. He did his little dance for me with appreciation.

Mom and Jack went straight to their spots—the couch and dining room chair—still in their swim clothes. They turned on the TV and settled in. I sat down on the floor, near Jack's feet so I could see the TV better and avoid the effects of Mom's chain smoking.

"You got a bit burned, huh?" Jack asked, his hand grazing the top of my back.

"I did?" I asked, craning my neck to try to see the marks the sun left on me.

"Grab me some lotion from your mom's stuff."

I jumped off the couch and dug in her bag. "This?" I asked, holding up a plain bottle of lotion. It's all I could find.

"That'll work." Jack reached for it.

"Are we going back to the pool? I like that Hawaiian Tropic lotion we use for swimming. It smells like summer!"

"No, but do you see this?" Jack dragged his fingers down my arm, goosebumps naturally rising in place from his cold touch colliding with my hot skin. "This is burned here, but this," he let his hand slide under the strap of my swimsuit, skimming the high swell of my only-starting-to-show chest, "this isn't burned. So, this is where we need to be sure we put the lotion."

"Why? I thought you put lotion on the burned part."

"No. That's only what fools believe. We put lotion on all the parts, but especially on the unburned area. The burned parts pull all the softness from those areas. We have to be sure they stay soft with lotion so they don't dry out. We can't have that happen now, can we?"

He turned the lotion bottle upside down, tapping it against his palm as the white creaminess slithered onto my skin. His hand moved about my body, rubbing small circles to large circles into my arms, my collarbone, my chest, my stomach, my legs.

I tensed, scared to move. I didn't want to further encourage it, but I also didn't want to make him angry. I didn't like it. Deep down, I could feel it wasn't right. I waited for my mom to tell him to stop.

My mom continued to stare at the TV, only feet away from me as her boyfriend freely touched her young daughter, putting lotion on parts that not even she had ever touched on me.

I tried to breathe, and I let my mind take me somewhere else far away. *This isn't my life. This is a movie. Just like on the TV.*

7

ALONE

*T*he environment at home had quickly turned volatile, but it became what I was used to facing each day. After a while, the numbness started to settle in. The only bits of reprieve came when I was at school and when my dad would pick me up on Sundays. Dad could tell that I wasn't happy with Jack and Mom, but he never pressed for details. He sat back, allowing me to speak when I wanted to, but I didn't. In such a heavily Mormon community, loyalty to your church and to your family is instilled everywhere. I didn't have a church, but I had family. Telling on Jack and Mom didn't feel right. Besides, I didn't have any friends to compare my life with. At that point, it was just life. It was a day-by-day experience. It wasn't me noticing that my life was different than what most of the others my age were experiencing. There were no social media displays showing the stark differences and signaling the warnings.

Dad was twenty-eight when he and Mom got divorced. Back then divorce was rare, especially in Utah. The children would always go to the mother. Dad didn't realize he could challenge that and have me with him full-time. I didn't know that either. If we did, things would have been different. But there's no point in thinking that way now.

I remember the first time I felt truly alone to such a degree that it shook my soul and left a scar that is still reflected in some of my reactions to this day.

I was nine-years-old and came home after school, opened the door, only to be greeted with silence. It wasn't completely uncommon. Some days Jack and Mom were home, and sometimes they stopped after work to pick up groceries or have a drink at a bar before coming home. They'd be here soon.

I turned on the living room light and said hi to Nino. Sneaking into the kitchen as though someone would care, I grabbed a few crackers to snack on. I flipped on the TV and found *The Jetson's*. I loved watching Jane Jetson on her shopping sprees. She would hurry home to try on her newest fashion accessory, and I was excited to see what she thought of it.

Once the show was over, Jack and Mom still weren't home.

"Where do you think they are?" I asked Nino. He chirped back a response I couldn't decipher.

Dusk fell. The house darkened. Night followed. I was still alone.

My stomach growled. They weren't going to be making me dinner. I searched the kitchen for what I could eat. Bologna. I reached for slimy slices of meat and added them to my plate. With the trembling butter knife in my hand, I spread mayonnaise on slices of bread. I pulled back the tab on a can of Spaghettios and dumped the messy sauce with a resounding plop on another plate. I thought I was hungry, but once I tried to take bites my stomach tossed and clenched, refusing to accept the food I was offering it like a toddler determined not to eat his vegetables.

What if something happened to them? What if they're hurt? What do I do if they are?

I sat near the phone, waiting for Jack or Mom to call, for someone to check in on me and tell me what's happening.

The minute hand on the clock ticked, one number after another in the deafening silence as it made rounds from one hour to the next.

I pushed my plates away and lay on the floor by the phone, waiting for it to ring. The garage doors beneath vibrated the floor and my body. With the sound of each one, I held my breath, waiting for their footsteps on the walkway.

No one.

Something must have happened to them.

Do I go to one of the neighbors for help? But it's dark. I can't be out there alone. That's scary.

Tears fell down my face as I hummed with Nino's songs to pass the time. Suddenly, the TV show that was humming in the background faded, and the American flag took over the screen. The national anthem played once, then the screen turned to a rainbow bar code. A very loud, high-pitched sound blared out of the box. I quickly ran over and turned the sound down, but kept the TV on just in case another show came on. Nothing did. I would soon learn that this was normal for TV in the 1970s. At midnight, the national anthem played and TV shows were gone for the night. I wasn't used to being up this late. Especially not alone.

Sleep must have won out because the door swinging open woke me out of my slumber sometime later. I sat up fully alert, fear greeting me as the moonlight poured in behind the shadowed bodies entering the apartment.

Mom and Jack tumbled in. Mom's perfect hairdo was matted with strings of auburn out of place. Jack's shirt was wrinkly with parts tucked in and parts undone. They could barely stand straight.

"What are you doing on the floor?" Mom yelled through slurs as though I couldn't hear her from only feet away. She always got louder with each drink she consumed. The count must have been high tonight.

"I didn't know where you were. I was scared," I admitted quietly.

"Well, we're here now, aren't we?" Jack said. "Get to bed!"

I moved to cover Nino's cage with the sheet and tell him goodnight, but Jack jumped in front of me.

"Didn't I say get to bed, you stupid dego?" he yelled, his spit droplets striking my face.

"Yes," I spoke calmly, walking on eggshells, not wanting to upset him more. "I just wanted to cover Nino's cage."

"You should have covered it at eight o'clock like you're supposed to. Now Nino will have to be awake all night. All because you are a stupid fucking wop. Now get to bed like I said!"

They left me alone for hours only to greet me by screaming at me as though I did something wrong.

Dragging my feet to the bedroom, I took one more glance behind me as Mom tugged her shirt over her head, getting undressed in the middle of the living room.

I put on my pajamas and crawled into bed, thankful it was over. *It was over.* They were back home. I wasn't alone. I'm not a wop- whatever that was. I was just scared.

When the morning sun poured into my room, I got out of bed and walked down the hall. Mom and Jack were sitting in their regular spots. Mom on the couch and Jack in his kitchen chair, twenty feet away from each other with eyes on the TV against the wall between them as they sipped coffee.

"Where were you guys last night?" I asked them.

"The Office," Jack replied, his eyes fixated on the TV.

I couldn't keep my voice from shaking. "I was scared. You don't usually stay at work that late."

Jack snickered without looking up still. "We weren't at work. We were at a bar called The Office. We work hard every fucking day. If we want to get a drink on the way home from work, we will."

Neither one acknowledged that I said I was scared. Neither one said anything about leaving me alone for such a long time, as though it wasn't a big deal.

But I knew it was. I was a child. I wasn't meant to be left alone.

Barely a week went by before the nightmare repeated itself. I came home from school. Jack and Mom weren't there. The fear hit immediately this time instead of slowly building up. I knew the threat that existed. They may not come back home for hours. I couldn't relax and watch TV. I just sat there perfectly still so I could hear every noise. Waiting.

With each garage door that opened, I would smile and say to Nino, "I bet that's them! I bet they're home!"

They weren't.

I poured myself cereal and sat on the floor, under the phone. I pushed the flakes around in the bowl with a spoon as they grew soggier in the milk. I struggled to take a bite. Eventually I dumped it in the sink, unable to eat.

The sky outside grew dimmer. I closed the curtains so no one could see me sitting in the apartment by myself.

It dawned on me how many people came into our

house with all the drinking parties Jack and Mom regularly threw. A stranger could come in at any point. I looked at Nino, wondering if he could protect me. Wishful thinking.

Shadows danced across the living room. The wind blew the stairs, making them jiggle and creak. Each time I ran into my room, waiting for it to pass, hoping it was only Jack and Mom coming and not some stranger.

Maybe they were on one of Jack's routes. If so, it could be four or five days before they returned. Would they leave me here that long?

Anything was possible.

The last time they were gone, Jack said they were at a bar.

What was the name? I couldn't remember. I squeezed my eyes, trying to recall what Jack said. I finally picked up the phone, cradling it close to me, and dialed 0 to ask the operator if she knew what bar was by my mom's work.

"No. I don't know who you are. I don't know your mom. I am sure she will be home soon though, it's dark out."

"I'm sure she will, too," I said, desperate to believe my words, grasping onto hope that if a random lady knew they should be home soon, that they would be.

I reached for the phone book, searching the yellow pages for the name of area bars. Dialing number after number, my heart raced as I asked for them to find my mom. "A short woman with red hair," I described.

"Nope, not here."

With each call, blaring rock music and excited voices in the background contradicted how I was feeling. I was alone in silence; others were having the time of their lives together. "Please don't hang up," I would pray, but it was trending. If they didn't see the woman I described, they hung up. No one wondered why a little girl on the other end was searching for her mom.

I looked at the clock. I knew it was late. Later than last time. The national anthem was long over. Nino was tired and tucked his head back into his wings, nodding off to sleep. I carefully covered him with the sheet and whispered goodnight. The silence used to bring me peace, but now, all I had was anxiety.

I lay on the floor, making sure I could answer the phone the moment they called and choked down the fear that they may never come back for me. They knew I was scared last time. They wouldn't do this again knowing that. Something had to have happened to them. They had to be hurt or in trouble.

THE OFFICE! I jolted up from a half-sleep. *That was the name of the bar!*

I found the number in the phone book. The guy who answered called out over the noise of the patrons in the background.

"I'm looking for my mom. Georgene."

"Yep, hold on."

Yes! She's there! I held my breath, waiting to hear my mom's voice.

The music and voices amplified. I imagined him setting the phone on the bar while he searched for my mom. Muffled voices mixed with the bass of a band were the only reply.

He never came back to the phone.

I cuddled the receiver closer, straining to recognize any of the voices.

"Hello? Hello?" I cried out.

Why wasn't he coming back to the phone?

I wrapped the cord around my finger, waiting, praying.

What if they're calling for me and can't get through?
I quickly hung up the phone so it could ring.
But it didn't.

I turned on the radio to wash out the eerie silence and provide extra noise. Then I turned it off so I could hear the phone if it rang. I could hear Nino dance around his cage as tears dripped down my face.

At least he was here. He was tired like me, but he wasn't sleeping. Was he scared too?

Maybe that's why they gave me the parakeets. To keep me company. Did they know they weren't going to be coming home each day?

More time passed as the tears fell.

I lay on the ground next to the phone, waiting, my stomach filling with trepidation. They were fine. They just weren't coming home for me.

They didn't care I was here alone.

I could call Dad, but if I did, he'd know Jack and Mom left me alone. Jack would be pissed that I tattled on him. Surely, they'd be back. Soon.

I drifted off to sleep, then woke up as the sun peeked through the curtains. All I could think about was the importance of washing my face and going to school. I didn't want to get in trouble. I was left alone and yet I was worried about getting in trouble. My stomach clenched as I thought about pouring a bowl of Captain Crunch and I realized I had no desire to eat still. Would anyone notice if I had the same clothes on as yesterday? I better at least put on a different shirt.

I made it through school in a fog. It used to be my break, but the anxiety gripped me the entire day. As I walked home from school, I was terrified about walking through the apartment door. What if they still weren't home? What do I do? Turning the knob, I bit my lip and prayed.

They weren't back. They had yet to be home.

Night after night, the same scene repeated. Left to be on my own at nine-years-old, never knowing when someone would return.

Why don't they care enough to let me know where they are?

As much as I would be relieved when they finally came through the door, I equally dreaded seeing them.

8

STRANGER SITTERS

King's Row was a huge apartment community. There were a lot of people living there, and for the most part, they all needed a little extra money.

Mom and Jack decided to take advantage of this. Maybe because they felt guilty or bad leaving me alone for days? Nah, probably not that. It was most likely because on the days they were home, before I left for school, I grilled them asking if they would be there when I got back. They knew I was scared. They always said they would be there.

Liars. They broke my trust bit by bit.

I'm sure the new process of hiring sitters every now and then started because they feared I would tell someone that they were leaving me alone for days at a time, and not for my own good. The same reason they didn't just let my Dad have me if they couldn't watch me.

The first time they had a stranger watch me, I remember taking a deep breath before opening the apartment door, a habit I had adopted after being alone the first time. I pushed open the door, clutching my schoolbooks tightly to my chest to see what I would be faced with. When it swung open, I exhaled. My mom was there, but she had my pink duffle bag in her hands.

"Let's go, you're staying with the neighbor lady tonight."

"Who?"

Mom waved her hand in the air, "I forget her name. You ask her."

I followed after her as she marched across the walkway and down the stairs toward another unit. "There," my mom pointed to the apartment.

"You're not coming with me?"

"She knows you're coming." Mom handed me the bag and turned to walk away without a goodbye or further instructions.

"How long are you leaving for?" I called out behind her, but she didn't turn around or answer.

I lifted my hand to knock on this unknown door and hesitated. Maybe I would be okay on my own. Maybe staying by myself was better than staying with strangers.

No. I had done that already. The vast emptiness I felt when not knowing if Mom and Jack were ever coming back was too much to bear. Now if they weren't, at least someone would see me and know that I've been left alone.

All I wanted was to be seen.

A lady with long bleach blonde hair and dull blue eyes opened the door. Her lipstick caught my attention the most, a beautiful mauve that I wondered if I could wear as well. Young kids, miniature skinny replicas of the woman ran around in circles behind her. I relaxed a little, until she said, "Hello?"

I looked behind me, but Mom was long gone. She must have gotten the apartment number wrong. I imagined having to knock on every door in the complex to find the one I was supposed to stay at instead. I bit my lip to keep it from quivering.

"My mom told me I was staying with you tonight." I held up my duffle bag as proof.

"Oh yeah, she gave me fifty dollars for that. Come on in."

I exhaled my relief and entered the apartment behind her. It was the exact layout of ours. How could so many kids fit in such a small space? The extra bodies made the air warmer.

I swiped at the sweat on my brow and stalled by the door, unsure what to do.

"Dinner is almost ready," the lady called from the kitchen while stirring a pot on the stove. "You can put your bag by the couch."

When Jack cooked, the aromas filled the room, tantalizing my stomach and sparking my curiosity for what was brewing. Even the roasted vegetables had a distinct, wonderful smell.

There was nothing in the air here despite the steam rising from her pot.

"Kids, dinner!" she called. Two girls and two boys between the ages of four and eight ran to the table. All had white hair like their mom. The boys had harsh bowl cuts while the girls' stringy hair was matted around their shoulders. They filed around the table and filled the chairs.

"Who's this?" a girl asked, wearily eyeing me.

"I don't remember her name," the lady said with a shrug. Apparently my name didn't matter. Just the fifty dollars. "Anyway, she lives down the way. She's staying with us for the night."

"Why?"

"Where's her mommy?"

Their mom shrugged again. I shrugged. No one knew where my mom was.

"Gina. My name is Gina," I said. *I'm a person. I'm worthy of acknowledgement.*

"Here you go," the lady scooped boiled macaroni into our bowls. She picked up an enormous can that was sitting on the table, punched a hole in the top and poured a small amount of watery red juice over each of our bowls of macaroni.

"Is this tomato juice?" I asked.

"What else would it be?" the lady retorted.

Sauce. Tomato sauce, I thought to myself.

I expected that the woman would provide bread or a side dish for more substance, but she didn't. She told us to eat up as she disappeared into her bedroom.

I poked at the macaroni. The kids around me devoured it, bowls almost empty within minutes as though they hadn't eaten all day.

A knock on the door. I sat up straight, wondering if my mom was coming back for me. The lady ran down the hallway to the living room and opened the door. A man with bleach blonde hair stood there instead. They exchanged a quick kiss, and he joined us at the table.

"This is Brent. He does construction." He must be her boyfriend.

"My dad is a construction worker," I told him, desperate for conversation.

"I thought your dad was a trucker?" Brent asked, looking over at the woman for confirmation.

"No. That's, um, my mom's boyfriend," I corrected him with a wince, hearing Jack's voice in my mind saying, "and um, you're dumb."

Brent didn't care that I said um. "Oh. Why aren't you staying with your Dad then?"

I looked back at my plate reluctantly and popped a hard noodle in my mouth, chewing slowly to avoid having to answer. I didn't know the answer to that.

I knew if my Dad knew I was being left with neighbors, he would have taken me. Why couldn't my mom just ask him to take me?

I slept on the couch, sinking into the cushions, feeling the springs beneath my body. Despite the lack of comfort, I was grateful knowing that people were around me and that I wasn't alone.

In the morning, I watched from the couch as the woman used a measuring cup and carefully measured a half-cup of cereal that she dumped into one bowl, gauging another half cup until she had covered the five bowls. She then measured a quarter cup of milk for each bowl, followed by a quarter cup of water for each of us. I've never seen someone make cereal with such accuracy. Or use water, for that matter.

"Breakfast is ready!" she called as she placed each bowl in front of us.

The first bite made me gag. Cereal is better on its own than with water on it. I tried to eat it because I was hungry. My stomach didn't knot up and prevent food from entering as much when other people were with me. Now it was just writhing, knowing what was coming down wasn't all that appetizing.

The kids didn't pay much attention to me. They were apparently used to other kids around, whereas for me, this was a novelty. I wasn't invited into the family, though. The woman barely talked to me. I was simply a paycheck.

I liked watching the kids' relationships together, how

they seemed to play and take care of each other. I wondered what it would be like to have siblings of my own.

I didn't give Mom much credit for handing me off to someone that first time she got a stranger to watch me, but I should have appreciated that moment more. Afterward, notes replaced her actually taking me to a new apartment.

It became routine. Coming home after school to a silent apartment. A note sitting on the kitchen counter scrawled in my mom's handwriting that said, "Go stay with the people in apartment 3B tonight." 3B? That's a new one. No specifics on where Mom and Jack were, when they were coming back, or who in the world I was staying with.

"Mom? Jack?" I called out, still expecting them to answer no matter how many times it happened.

Silence.

I shivered as I hurried to my bedroom. I didn't want to be left alone again.

At least I wouldn't be alone tonight, even if I had no clue who these people were. Grabbing my Barbie duffle bag, I stuffed it with clothes, my toothbrush, and coloring books. The last time they left me with someone, it was for four days. I packed enough to expect that again.

Closing the door behind me and locking it, I leaned over the railing, trying to determine where 3B would be.

The walkways in the search for 3B felt endless. I might never be able to find the right number. *What if she wrote it down wrong? What if there's no 3B? What if the people have no clue I'm coming? What if I'm going to end up alone?*

Finally, there it was. The brown door of 3B.

I knocked, wondering who was going to be on the other side of this one.

The door swung open, and I gasped. A lady with dark

skin. I had seen a few people with brown skin in my life, Hispanics or Pacific Islanders, not a black person.

Jack hated people of color. I heard it all the time. I must have the wrong apartment. There's no way he would have allowed this.

"Gina," the lady said with a warm smile. "I was starting to get worried about whether you would find us."

She was worried about me?

The lady took a step back and opened the door wider, so I could come through. I stepped past her, and my stomach grumbled loudly. I didn't grab a snack at the house, and I was hungry. The scents coming from her kitchen were enticing—meat and potatoes roasting in the oven.

"I'm Octavia, and this is Henry," she pointed to the living room where a tall man with broad shoulders waved. He also had dark skin.

"Nice to meet you, Gina." His voice was deep and he had kind eyes that wrinkled at the corners.

"Come on now. Let's take your bag to your room."

"I have my own room?" I asked.

Octavia looked at me with a sad smile. "You think we'd let you sleep on the couch? Of course not. Besides, it's just me and Henry here. We never got around to having kids. The spare bedroom is yours."

She opened the door to the second room and let me get situated as though it was my own. She made it clear she wasn't just watching me, but she wanted me to truly feel at ease. I wasn't used to strangers going out of their way for me.

After dinner, I sat in a chair while Octavia and Henry sat on the couch and watched TV. No one talked, but it was comfortable. I liked it. I didn't feel strange going to bed. I didn't feel out of place. In fact, it was the best I had felt in a while.

I was awakened in the morning by a whiff of sautéed onions. *Is Octavia cooking? Who makes hot breakfast on school days?* It was such an abnormal concept for me.

I got dressed and walked into the kitchen. "What's this?"

Octavia placed a plate at an open seat. It was filled with scrambled eggs and potatoes mixed with onions and tiny pieces of green bell peppers. "Breakfast. Don't you eat breakfast? The meal of champions."

"But I have school today."

"You still gotta eat. You can't make it through without a solid meal. Sit on down."

I nodded and obeyed, struggling to communicate that I wasn't used to a home-cooked breakfast before school. It wasn't in my scope of expectations. Cold cereal was daily. Lately, sometimes mixed with water when I stayed with the bleached-hair lady and her kids.

I took a bite and melted into the savory deliciousness. "This... is... amazing," I managed to say between mouthfuls.

Octavia nodded with her coffee cup pressed to her lips. Her smile was hidden, but I could tell cooking compliments were her favorite.

I walked to school with a full belly, amazed that a stranger cared enough to make me such a good meal just to start my day off right.

After staying with them, each time I walked through our apartment door to see a note on the table, I got excited. I ran to it, hoping to see 3B again. I like Octavia and Henry! I wanted to stay there more than anything.

Instead, a new one was scribbled on there. 5A. Where do they even meet these people? They rarely socialized outside of the apartment. I could see Jack and Mom knocking on doors, waving bills until someone was willing to take their brat of a daughter.

Deflated, I filled my bag, turned off the lights of the empty apartment and locked the door. Somehow, this had become my new normal.

I wasn't as scared to knock on the new door, although I still wondered who was on the other side.

This time, a man closer to Jack's height but mom's age, opened the door. "Hey," he greeted as he rubbed his glasses on his shirt and put them back on his face.

He was nice enough and even made me pizza for dinner. I slept on the couch. He was the least experienced with watching a child and wasn't sure how to keep me entertained—which was fine, I had learned to do that all on my own. But now as an adult, thinking about them leaving me with a strange man they didn't know turns my stomach. It was clear that Jack and Mom had no standards about what qualified someone to watch me. As long as they were guilt-free that was all that mattered.

I don't remember how many families I stayed with over the years. There were many more than mentioned here. I stayed with the bleach blond family several times, probably because she needed the money. But the others, I only stayed with one time each. I never got to go back to Henry and Octavia's despite their warm welcome. I get it; I wasn't theirs. I would hear all of them murmuring, asking when Mom was going to be back to pick me up. Jack and Mom were never back when they told the people they would be. They would freely disappear without accountability and responsibility, living as though there wasn't a child waiting for them back home.

It didn't feel like I belonged anywhere. Ever since the divorce, any sense of security was being stripped away bit by bit. It started with Dad, my saving grace, no longer in our house. Then my few friendships ending over not following typical Mormon standards. The move from our house in Bountiful to the apartment in King's Row and being even further away from my Dad was a terrible adjustment. Jack and Mom's constant actions suggesting I'm not important and only a hindrance to the lifestyle they craved. Then the increasing debilitating fear of Jack's anger and unwelcomed touches.

Even something as simple as walking home from school each day lost its enjoyment. The questions and anxiety ransacked my mind. Would Jack and Mom be home? If so, what kind of terror awaited me? If they weren't home, would they come home? If there was a note, where would I be and would I be safe there?

I'm still amazed that none of the people who I stayed with ever hurt me. It was a huge apartment complex and Mom was desperate to throw her child into the hands of anyone who would say yes. There's no doubt God was watching out for me, keeping the doors closed to anyone else that could have done worse.

9

FAMILY & HOLIDAYS

*B*y the time I was ten-years-old, I was unsure where I belonged, lost in the transitional voids of the unfamiliar and absence of home. So, when invites arose to visit the houses of other family members, I seized them. I loved leaving Mom and Jack's to go see other family. I didn't get to very often. Any chance to be somewhere else was welcomed.

Like Grandma Judd's house. She was my dad's mom. I'd be dropped off at her house, and she would hug me in a warm embrace, taking my bag from my hands.

"I had a lot of ladies today, so I'm just getting home. Go down to the basement and say hi to Grandpa Judd while I get all this hair dye off of me and change my clothes." She worked as a hair stylist and would regularly smell of hair chemical mixed with roses.

Grandpa Judd was in the family room of the dark basement smoking his pipe. I breathed in the incredible scent of tobacco leaves as I leaned down to hug him. He was my grandma's second husband. Her first husband, my Grandpa

Defa, died when my dad was nine-years-old. I didn't get the chance to know him, but Grandma kept his spirit alive with stories about his Italian family and the ranch they lived on.

"Can I ride my bike to the store?" I just got here and I was already ready for the open-air freedom. Just to know I was free of Jack and Mom and still cared for by people who loved me was liberating.

"That's a little too far to go alone, Gina. Besides the road is too busy for a little girl to be on by herself."

Mom let me ride my bike on that road all the time when we lived in Bountiful. She never said it wasn't safe.

"I bet you'd like to go pick out a paint by numbers or a new coloring book. Come on, I'll drive you up there."

That man got me. I was pumped to have new art supplies.

Grandpa Judd waited in the car for me as I ran into the store and found a new paint by numbers. The one with a dog lying down on the grass grabbed my attention. It looked hard. Perfect! I wasn't one to back down from a challenge.

When we returned to the house, Grandma warmed up a pot of her red sauce and boiled spaghetti noodles, adding green beans and a roll to the side of the plate. She loved to cook and passed down her skills to me, demonstrating how to make various dishes when I came to stay. Italian meals were her specialty. Even though she wasn't Italian, Grandpa Defa's mom taught her how to make all his favorite meals when they were first married. She liked to grow her own vegetables in the tiny backyard garden. My favorite was the comfrey she grew. She would make me a morning shake with comfrey, her own canned peaches, and sunflower seeds. It was her secret recipe and absolutely delicious. I never had anything like it before.

Grandma and Grandpa Judd asked me how school was

going and told me about projects they had going on around the house. We had a real conversation that I didn't realize I was craving until it took place. It had been a while since someone last asked questions about me. At night, I lay my head on a comfy pillow in the extra bedroom where I always got to sleep. I waited patiently for the train horn in the distance. Listening to it blow, I breathed in deep and relaxed. It became my signal of comfort, confirming I was here, in my grandma's house, safe from the dark chaos of my own home. I was far away from Jack and my mom, back in loving hands.

My greatest and most normal memories from childhood were usually from time spent with my extended family members.

One summer, Jack was scheduled to have several more truck trips than usual, and my mom didn't want to miss out on going with him. They put me on a plane to fly to Kelso, Washington, to stay with my other grandma, my mom's mom. My grandma loved having me and would always tell my mom, "Just send her on up here."

It was beautiful in Kelso. Grandma Walker's trailer was surrounded by bright flowers and a little pond with giant goldfish in it. We would sit for hours and watch the big fish lazily swim around the pond, stopping to look up as if asking us for some dried fish flakes. We could only feed them once a day but when they saw me standing there, they expected a meal no matter the time of day.

Staying active was very important to Grandma Walker. She liked to walk the length of her street, up to her mailbox, chatting with her neighbors as we passed their homes. We walked to the blackberry bushes that ran down the edges of the back entrance of the trailer park. Grandma Walker taught me how to carefully reach in and pick the berries, being extra careful not to get pricked by their sharp thorns. I'd reach in, feeling my fingers connect with a big berry. Excitement would shoot through me and I'd pull my arm out too fast, snagging my shirt on a bramble. Grandma would patiently unhook me from the vine, take me home and sew up the snag I created. It wouldn't have been such a calming affair back at home. Mom would have yelled and sent me to my room for ripping my clothes on accident. Many reasons why I was grateful to be miles upon miles away from home.

I loved roller skating at the rink just down the street from Grandma Walker's trailer park. She even joined me, once, which is all it took for her to fall and break her arm. I felt so bad, but she just laughed. She had the best laugh! She said she would rather try to skate and break her arm more than just sit around at home doing nothing.

Since Grandma Walker didn't like to cook, she would let me create meals. I discovered you could make a grilled cheese sandwich in the waffle iron. When she said it was the best meal she had ever had, of course I had to make it every day that I was there. I pretended I was a waitress taking her order. She played along, asking for a waffle iron grilled cheese with a Sprite and a dessert of shortbread cookies or the banana bread we made earlier in the week.

By the time Jack and Mom picked me up from the airport after my visit with Grandma Walker, my mom looked at me with disgust. "You're fat!"

I pulled at the waistband of my jeans, which were noticeably tighter than when I first left.

"Why are you so fat?" she pressed for answers.

I hung my head. I had one of the best summers of my life. The fun was replaced with guilt, like I did something I shouldn't have done. "I learned how to cook," I answered. I was proud of it, or had been prior to Mom's comment.

"Looks like you learned how to eat," Mom said with a sneer.

Jack grunted. "I cook in our house. Not you. Got it?"

I nodded and followed them out of the airport, back to reality.

Mom complained all the way home. She was embarrassed that I looked like I did, which I didn't know was any different than I looked before. Suddenly I was aware of what fat might mean, and that apparently it was a bad thing. When all I did was try to be good to appease everyone, one thing after another backfired and every decision seemed to make me even more of a disgrace to Jack and Mom.

Two to three times a year, I stayed with my Aunt Janet who offered to take care of me on the weekends. She was my mom's sister, raised in the same house with the alcoholic and abusive father. But Janet was opposite of my mom. She was incredibly kind and took a liking to me. I think she always knew more than she let on about what I was experiencing at home. Single and overweight, she had a different way of carrying her difficult upbringing than my mom.

Aunt Janet worked at a dentist's office and since the office was closed on the weekends when I visited, she snuck me in. Pretending she needed something from her desk, she pulled out the toy box filled with prizes for kids who had been good during their appointment.

"Pick one, and only one!" she instructed with joy.

"Ooh!" I squealed as I browsed the selection. It was so hard to pick just one!

After the office visit, we went to the store so she could stock up on her number one addiction, TAB. We'd leave with Aunt Janet waddling out, the twenty-four pack of soda in her thick hand, knocking her off balance.

Janet was different than other adults I had been around, which is why I liked her. She wasn't in a relationship until much later in life. Pure goodness oozed out of her, shining through her eyes and in every action she made. She diligently worked, paid her bills, and didn't overspend. Janet lived a frugal, quiet life, but she was loving and protective of those she allowed herself to get close to.

Jack was excluded from that. Janet often commented how bossy he was, saw through him early on and openly stated that Jack was a bad choice for my mom. Jack didn't like Janet either, slinging around insults about her weight and how no man would ever marry her. "The old maid of the family," he called her.

Janet held out two TV dinner options in front of me. This was also the norm when I stayed with her. I made my selection, and she warmed it up for me. We sat in her living room watching game shows, eating on TV stands. It was cool, and I loved it.

"Shh, I'm not supposed to give this to you," she said with a wink as she handed me the icy cold TAB can. I let the fizz settle before I took a sip.

Janet asked how things were going at home, and I gave the standard answer that I gave everyone, "Fine." Guilt gnawed at me with the temptation to badmouth my mom and Jack. Janet must have known that home life wasn't good. She made sure to never be around Jack. The few times she was forced to be around him, she spoke up, pushed back at Jack like few people ever would. She didn't stand for being talked down to. She was also quite protective of me.

I dreaded returning home after my glorious getaways with family members. Two years of Jack in my life, and he was becoming more unpredictable than ever. My mom was a bit more unsurprising, but not in a good way. Cigarettes, alcohol, TV, parties, and avoiding mothering were her standard operating procedures. Jack always seemed to be looking for more, and his "more" was usually filled with dark, not light.

After Aunt Janet dropped me off at home, I came through my bedroom door and walked straight into a drunk Jack. "Your room is a goddamn mess," he slurred, throwing my clothes around the room. "You never do a goddamn thing around here!"

He picked up a pile of my clothes and walked them to the front door, throwing them over the banister and onto the carport below.

"Jack, stop! I'll clean!" I hurried and reached for some clothes to fold and put in my drawer.

Jack stormed back into my room and grabbed my coloring books before pivoting on his heel and heading to the front door again. I ran after him, pleading with him to stop. I watched in horror as the pages flew over the banister and scattered across the concrete like the fate of my clothes.

I ran to the phone and dialed my dad. "Dad! Jack is throwing all my clothes and stuff over the banister! He's mad at me for not cleaning my room!"

"I'll be right there," Dad said before being cut off by the dial tone.

"Who are you talking to, you fucking brat?" Jack jeered.

"My dad, he's coming to get me."

Jack rolled his eyes, continuing his stampede to my room, grabbing more of my items, and dropping them over the banister. "Good, your goddamn Dad can have you! Two dego wops – you are perfect for each other!"

Nino squawked at him, and he turned his attention to

my poor little parakeet. "And this smelly thing! You can't even clean your room, you sure as hell can't take care of a bird!" Jack grabbed for the cage, his misplaced anger absolutely terrifying.

"No! Not Nino!" I begged him. "I'll clean! I'll clean my room and his cage!" I didn't care about my clothes, but Jack couldn't hurt Nino, my only true friend, my companion every single day, the one constant I had.

"Stop," another voice interrupted the nightmare unfolding.

Jack jerked his head up. I was shocked to see my dad standing there. He made it in record time from his place to ours.

"Your lazy bitch of a daughter doesn't do shit around here."

In a flash, Dad closed the front door and was across the room hovering over Jack in the corner of the living room. I stood against the wall on the other side with wide eyes as my dad's arm pressed against the base of Jack's neck.

My dad had the kindest blue eyes with a continual smile shining in them. Now the emotion drained out of them with nothing but rage pulsating as he towered over Jack.

"She will get her things and put them back in her room. And you don't ever, *ever* touch her bird. You hear me?"

I steadied my breathing, knowing everything would be okay. Dad was only a call away and would be there in an instant if I needed him. It took that moment for it to sink in that in all the chaos of my life, Dad was indeed there for me —more than just on Sundays.

As Thanksgiving that year neared, Jack and Mom went on another one of his trips. I was excited because I wanted to be with Dad for Thanksgiving, so it was perfect timing.

"You're staying with someone else," my mom informed me.

"What? Why can't I stay with Dad?" It made no sense. It was a holiday. A time to be with family. I should be with my dad. They weren't going to be around anyway

"I've already arranged this. Let's go." She had my bag in her hands.

"But it's Thanksgiving. I want to be with Dad," I tried to reason as I followed her. My dad had just told me last Sunday that he would love to spend Thanksgiving with me. He wanted me. He would let me stay with him.

"We'll be back in time for Thanksgiving dinner. It's my holiday, not your dad's."

In other words, this was all about her pride, and not about what was best for me.

Two buildings later, we were standing in front of the door that belonged to the bleach blonde family.

I turned to my mom, knowing how this usually ended. Me overstaying my welcome because Jack and Mom didn't keep their promise on the time they would return. "You're picking me up for Thanksgiving, right?" I was all but pleading with her. I didn't want to eat watered down tomato noodles for the holiday.

"Yes," Mom rolled her eyes. "Give her this." Mom stuck cash in my hands to pay off the lady to watch me and left without another word.

Thanksgiving morning rolled around, and I was still at the neighbor's house. I sat on the couch with my bag, waiting for my mom, watching as the kids made paper turkeys. The lady was cooking in the kitchen while Brent sat at the table and drank a beer. It was obvious she was agitated. I thought at first she was frustrated about cooking a full dinner because the air was actually filled with similar aromas as Octavia's or my grandmas' house for once. Then I realized it wasn't about the dinner, but about my presence there.

I just kept thinking, *this is what Thanksgiving should look like. Homemade cooking surrounded by family.* As usual, I was watching the movie of someone else's life instead of experiencing it in my own.

My homesickness for my Dad grew, my stomach clenching in response. My stomach had started being the depository for my anxiety.

"I'm just going to go see if they're back yet," I told the lady.

She nodded in response, her perfectly painted lips pressed in a thin line.

I ran down to my apartment, turning the key to open it. Hope glimmered inside that maybe Jack and Mom were cooking a big turkey and wanted to wait for it to be done before they picked me up.

I opened the door, excited for the Thanksgiving smells promising a delicious meal to come.

The lights were still off. The air was still. No one had been here for days. I returned to the neighbor's apartment with slumped shoulders. Hers slumped too when she realized I was still her responsibility.

I took four more trips to check to see if Jack and Mom were there, each time believing that Thanksgiving turkey dinner was only moments away. Surely, they were planning something special.

When Jack and Mom finally showed up, the lady was beyond agitation to anger. "Take your kid. We're trying to have *our* family holiday. You said you would be back yesterday and here we are, a few hours from Thanksgiving dinner and you are just now showing up? Really?"

That was the last time I stayed there.

Yet another bridge burned that I had no control of.

Jack and Mom walked me back to the apartment, cursing about the lady's rudeness. I ignored them, simply excited to see the size of the turkey that would be sitting on the table. When we opened the door, there was... nothing. No cooking. No groceries on the counter. No apologies that they showed up late on Thanksgiving Day to finally get me.

"Aren't we making Thanksgiving dinner?"

"Nope! This year, I have a fun surprise for you," Mom said with a grin.

This is weird. Mom never acted like this, but I rolled with it. She said she would be home for Thanksgiving, and she was. Maybe not when I thought she would be, but maybe she's actually trying to make it special. Maybe she had planned this surprise the whole time.

By the time we got loaded in the car, I was pumped and singing to the radio. We drove down the highway before taking an unfamiliar exit and parked in front of Benihana, a Japanese steakhouse. Jack and Mom got out of the car, and I hesitantly followed, still holding onto hope that there would be a traditional Thanksgiving meal at the end of this.

Instead, we watched the hibachi grill fire up.

I stared at the chopped vegetables and chicken pushed around by the chef on the hot grill. Jack and Mom were lost in their drinks, oblivious to the little girl they dragged along, sitting in a pool full of disappointment. My stomach ached, and I choked back tears. I thought about all my birthdays and the holidays that I didn't get to celebrate because my mom's personal agenda ran the show. She had the chance to let me celebrate Thanksgiving with my Dad and his family. Except she discarded me at a stranger's house until the last possible moment and replaced Thanksgiving with chopsticks. Then she pretended like it was something special, as though I couldn't see through her disillusioned words to the truth of her actions.

While my trust in my Mom had been slowly waning, that day it disappeared forever, going up in the same flames charring our Japanese vegetables.

10

TABLE GYMNASTICS

*J*ack's corruptions only became more obvious the older I became. Instead of revealing them all at once, he pulled back the curtain bit by bit. I went from being in the audience watching his antics to becoming more of the show.

After another trip the pool, Jack sat at his favorite plastic-covered chair at the oblong dining room table. I walked out of my bedroom after changing into clothes from my swimsuit, curious what was for dinner.

"Gina, you're all burned again. Grab the lotion."

I did as I was told, dragging my feet, knowing what was coming.

I glanced at my mom before crawling onto his lap, leaning against his shirt, feeling the cigarettes from his front pocket press against my back. His polyester pants stuck to my bare legs as my feet dangled just above his dirty brown boots.

We watched the TV for a while as he rubbed the lotion over my arms and legs. His plump fingers slid under my shirt to get the lotion in the areas untouched by the sun, so the burn wouldn't spread.

Jack suggested, "Want to have some fun?"

"Sure!" Fun was a rarity in the house, and I was a bit overeager at the idea of it.

"Great, jump down. Stand up on your feet. Turn your body and face me."

I did as he directed.

"Now come back up on my lap." I began to turn back around. *Why would he have me get off his lap just to get back on?*

"Gina! What are you doing? Turn back around."

"You said get back on your lap."

"Yes, this way," he sighed, exasperated. "Come here, give me your right leg."

He grabbed my ankle, pulling it up and onto the side of his leg, causing me to lose my balance from the force of the tug. He laughed and caught my flailing arm.

"I got you. Come on now."

Moving my legs on either side of him, I straddled his thighs and put my hands on his shoulders so I was looking directly into his face. "Okay." I said as he shifted me around in his lap.

"You trust me?" he asked, his blue eyes shining.

I didn't, but I just shrugged playfully in response.

"Let go of my shoulders and lean all the way back," Jack coached.

I looked behind me at the distance to the floor and back at him.

"I've got you," he repeated, his grip on my legs tightening. "You won't fall. It'll be fun."

So I did it. I leaned back while he held onto my thighs. I put my hands on the floor as though I was doing a backbend. "Good!" he encouraged, and I ate up his approval. He was right, this was fun!

"Okay, now.... Go!" He threw my legs over my head. My body flipped backward, and I landed on my knees facing him. I was stunned, until I realized the awesome move that I just did.

"Wow!" Not naturally athletic, the blood was pumping through my veins and my ego suddenly screamed out, "Yes! I can do gymnastics!" *Here I am, doing them! Olympics, here I come!* No longer was I Gina, but I was a beautiful gymnast, training for my next competition.

"Again!" I returned to his lap, eager to repeat it.

"Try this," Jack said, encouraging me to lean even further and bend my back more.

We did one backbend after another. I was learning how to stand up right away afterward, like the gymnasts did on TV as they shot their hands in the air to celebrate. He was right—it was the most fun we had in the apartment so far.

"This is so great!" I yelled out as I nailed my landing.

Moving back to climb up in his lap again for what I knew would be my best landing yet, Jack casually said, "Next time, we should do it with our clothes off."

"Huh?" I straightened my back and took my hands off his shoulders, confused, wondering if I heard him right. "Why would we do that?"

"Because it would make it a lot more fun. Don't you think?" Jack said nonchalantly, as though it was a common statement and not at all inappropriate. Staring at him, unsure if it was safe to answer, I paused.

"Next time, no clothes." He repeated with something different sparking in those icy eyes of his.

I did our table gymnastics flip one more time, with clothes on, just to appease him. I knew if I stopped right then, he would have noticed that he said something wrong. I knew better than to poke the bear. His anger was scary period; it was worse when someone made him feel wronged.

I didn't crawl back on Jack's lap again. I glanced at my mom, sitting only feet away, watching the TV as though nothing weird had just happened. I grabbed crackers and an orange from the kitchen despite my stomach turning in knots, just to pretend I had a different intention than running away from Jack so he wouldn't get suspicious. I walked into my room, shutting the door quietly, my heart beating hard against my chest.

What just happened?

11

MICE, TEDDIES, & POLAROIDS

henever I was in the room with them I tried to avoid looking at Jack and Mom as they sat on the couch together. Jack didn't sit next to her often, but when he did, he had his arm slung over her neck and his hands down her shirt. He always wanted to see and play with her boobs and didn't care who saw him do it. It didn't matter if she was walking by him or he was sitting by her, he would reach out and pull her shirt up, or down, whichever was the easiest way to expose her chest. Sometimes he just looked and smiled. Sometimes he grabbed her. And sometimes he put her boob in his mouth and sucked on it for a while.

If I sat next to them, Jack would slip his fingers under the cloth of my shirt, my pants, my swimsuit. If I started to move away, he would put his hand on my thigh, tightly. I knew not to move when that happened. Even while his leg connected with my mom's as they sat on the couch, he'd let his hands roam over me with no concerns that he'd be caught.

Mom ignored it.

I tried to sit on the floor when I could. When he didn't summon me to the couch, that is.

One time, Jack got up to refill his drink and crouched down next to me on the floor on his way back. "We're going to do something really fun. Want to play a game?"

The last time he said we were going to have fun, it wasn't. Well, the table gymnastics were fun, but he had to dirty it like he dirties everything. My kid hope still fluttered, though. Sometimes I wondered if any of the other kids had adults that actually played with them, or how it'd be to have a brother and sister to spend the days with.

"Yes," I said, hesitant but hopeful.

"Good." He waved my mom over. She rose from the couch and shifted her shorts to sit down next to me on her knees, complacent as always.

"Go get your mom's brown eye pencil," he directed me.

Are they going to let me wear makeup? I ran to the bathroom and located her eye pencil immediately, holding it up in the air as I trotted back like it was an award.

"Good girl," Jack cooed as he pulled the clear thin cap off the eye pencil. "Did you know you have a mouse in your shirt?"

I laughed at the thought.

"No, you do. It's a sweet little mouse with a tiny pink nose. Want to meet it?"

"No..." I answered, wondering how a mouse in my shirt was fun. If anything, it was weird. I knew Nino would definitely not want a mouse around the house. I looked up at him. He was stretching a leg on the swing, looking bored with the conversation. He turned his back to us and began to fluff himself out. I wish I could turn Jack out so easily.

"Take off your shirt," Jack said.

That's not what I expected to hear.

I looked at my mom, but she was focused on Jack, sipping her drink.

"Go on now," he said.

"No, I don't want to."

"Aww, come on! I promise it will be fun."

"No." I stood firm.

"Okay, I tell you what—I'll show you your mom's mouse first, then we can find yours." He turned to my mom. "Take your shirt off so we can show Gina how fun the mice are." She did as she was told without hesitation.

A robot.

Jack moved in close to Mom's chest and dragged the rough edge of the eye pencil point across her fair skin. "There," he said when he was finished. "Look at the cute mouse."

I stared at my mom's bare chest, trying to make sense of it. Her nipple was the nose. A line was drawn from the nose down into an upward curve of a smile with teeth bared inside. Whiskers dotted the side of the nose, her nipple, with two little eyes squinting above it.

"Here, you help me draw the other one."

I was guilty of enjoying drawing and the mouse face was cute, if you didn't think about where it was being drawn. My hand shook as I shoved aside the awkwardness of drawing on my mom's breast and the fear of what would happen if I told Jack no.

Jack covered my hand holding the eye pencil with his hand. He lifted the mouseless one of my mom's large breasts with his other hand until her nipple pointed straight at me. Guiding the eye pencil and my hand, he "helped" me turn my mom's breast into a matching mouse to the other one.

"You're a great artist! All that time in your room coloring is paying off."

I blushed. I couldn't help it despite the unease in the pit of my stomach. They rarely complimented me. I craved their affirmation.

Then Jack turned the tables again. "Okay, your turn. Shirt off."

I didn't want to do this. Oh, how I didn't want to do this. I looked at my mom, silently pleading for her help. My mom stared back, the demanding message obvious. *Do what Jack says. Now.*

I moved my eyes to Jack's big, pitted nose only inches away from my body. He leaned in to grab the hem of my shirt and lifted it up over my head.

I shivered in the chill of the air.

Mother and daughter, sitting side-by-side, topless in front of Jack. He picked up the eye pencil and started his next drawing.

I looked up at the ceiling, ignoring Jack's breath on my breast, wondering why my mom was allowing it. Only minutes long, but it felt like hours, like it would never end.

Finally, Jack sat back, admiring his creation. "Check that out, Gina."

I looked down to see a smaller version of my mom's mice on my innocent ten-year-old body. Mom was looking too. *What was she thinking? Isn't this wrong?* Blank eyes. No reaction. No words.

Jack kissed her breasts and rubbed his nose on her nipples—I mean, against the mouse nose, when he was finished. I froze, hoping he wouldn't do the same to mine.

Jack applauded his artwork. "Mama mouse and baby mouse. How cute," he mused. "That may be my best work yet. Twins."

He stood up and left the room. I stayed near my mom,

afraid to move. She sat there as though nothing was wrong and took a sip of her Black Velvet and Coke.

Jack soon returned with his camera. "Smile, mousey, mousey." He took one picture. Then another. And another. Moving closer, *click, click*. Moving further away, *click, click*. Both of us, mother and daughter, sitting in the middle of the living room topless with mice drawn on our breasts.

At some point I left my body, watching this all unfold from the sidelines. This wasn't my life. This was a movie I was an unfortunate spectator to. *Not real life. Not my life. I'm more than this.*

Unfortunately, that wasn't the last of the mice. Jack loved his mice drawings and his photography of them afterward.

As soon as I had permission, I shimmied my shirt back over my head.

Jack had an obsession with making me into my mom. Matching clothes with her was another way he went about it.

"Here, this is for you." Mom handed me a shopping bag, yet another present after they had been gone for a week.

Another shirt, I thought. *Always a t-shirt.* The last two times the shirt matched the one my mom had on. I didn't like the matching part. I was a kid. I liked kid clothes.

I opened the bag. It wasn't a shirt this time.

"What is this?" I held up the thin lace in my hands, trying to sort it out into a shirt or pants or anything at all that made sense.

"It's a nightgown. There are two, one for you and one for your mom. Twins." Jack breathed out cigarette smoke into the air, a twisted smile on his lips.

I tried to untangle the thin fabric. Purple and black lace entwined together. Something fell to the ground, and I jumped back. Did I break it? It was too small to be a night-gown. I picked it up and evaluated it closer. Underwear? But you could see through the sheer fabric. It couldn't be under-wear. Underwear covers. This didn't look like my underwear.

"Go put it on so we can see if it fits." Jack pointed to the bedroom.

"This?" I asked, incredulous that they were being seri-ous. "Is it a costume?"

"Come on, Gina." Mom said as she took the material out of my hands and headed toward her bedroom. "You get the black one. I like the purple."

I stood next to my mom and tried to mimic her moves as she slipped into the garment. Her movements were much more graceful than mine. She clearly had more experience wearing these things. I still didn't know what it was. The lace pressed against my skin, revealing parts of myself that a swimsuit wouldn't even show. I wouldn't be wearing this to the pool or anywhere. "I think mine has holes in it." I tried to peek in the mirror but she shoved me out of the bedroom before I could see it in full view.

When we were out in the light, standing in the living room in front of Jack, I finally saw how my mom looked. My heart dropped in the pit of my stomach, the shame of knowing we matched.

"What is this?" I asked, still pulling at the uncomfortable lace.

"Nice." Jack gruffed, evaluating us, his chilly eyes going from our legs to our chests. "It's called a teddy. Get used to it. This is what girls wear to look nice."

I didn't want to wear mine anymore, especially the way Jack's eyes clouded over as he watched us. Me in the black, my mom in the purple. Me as a ten-year-old, my mom as a thirty-two-year-old.

I reached for my teddy bear as Jack paraded us out into the middle of the living room. My teddy bear was crocheted, soft, sweet—a reminder of good things existing outside of this dark and scary house. I held the toy tightly as I looked down to see my bare legs and most of my bare tummy. The inverted lace "V" cut just covered my chest and sides.

Jack left the room and came back with his Polaroid camera. I froze next to my mom. I hated that camera. *Click.* The picture slid out of the base. *Click.* Another photograph. *Click.* More, dropping to the floor. I could feel the energy of bad, dark thoughts coming from Jack. With every step he took to get closer to us, I hugged my bear tighter, and removed myself from existing.

I'm watching a movie... it's not real life... this is not my life.
Click.

Another day alone in the house after school, I walked around, searching for clues of where Jack and Mom may have run off to this time, and whether they were coming back or not. There was no note, no hint of their trip. Only a darkening night sky.

I entered their bedroom and flipped on the light, looking to see if they took their overnight bag or not. I dragged my hand across their bedroom furniture, feeling the sense of extra corruption here. My eyes traveled to the dresser drawer.

Snooping wasn't allowed. Jack wouldn't have liked it. But a closed dresser drawer was like a chest of treasures for a child, something to explore. Maybe to play dress up with.

I opened up the first one, a narrow drawer on the top row—and immediately wished I hadn't.

A mountain of Polaroids taken from Jack's camera filled the long drawer. Hundreds of photos documenting years of his filthy photography hobby. My mom was his primary model. Sometimes she had clothes on, most of the times she didn't. Some with her legs open, spread wide for the camera. Some with my mom being penetrated by men that I didn't recognize, bodies different than that of Jack's. He's always the one with the camera. He was the photographer.

I closed the drawer and ran out of the room, wishing I had never seen proof of what I already knew existed.

If her photos were in there, where were the ones of me? Hidden further inside, or somewhere else?

I determined right then that I would never let him take another picture of me again.

The next time he tried, I said "no."

He didn't push it.

I wondered if my mom ever said no.

12

PARTIES & BILL

*T*here were always warning signs of an impending party. Oh, how I hated those parties. I hated leaving Nino out in them. Jack would buy several half gallons of whiskey to add to the one that regularly sat on the kitchen counter. My mom would clean the apartment. Vacuuming was definitely a sign that a party was about to go down. She would also cover her favorite table with a tablecloth. We never used this table, other than to host the massive, round, green, glass lamp that sat on it. But the lamp would come off and be replaced by a tablecloth that draped all the way to the floor. Coasters were plopped on top that. Now that the table was protected, it was party time.

The parties were regular occurrences in the apartment. Any day. Anytime. Unpredictable. Loud rock music shook the walls. They happened after Jack and Mom's workdays and on the weekends. People they met at the swimming pool and the grocery store, their truck driver friends who were in town, whoever they knew all came over with arms laden of alcohol. I wish they could have waited until I was at my Dad's or send me over there when the parties were happening, but if that was the case, I would have been at my dad's three times per week.

The party prep was my sign to stay locked in my room and out of the way. I tried my best to stay out of the way—in my room at the end of the hallway. I did not want to be part of the party. Loud drunks have never been my thing. The rock music they played terrified me as it pounded the walls. AC/DC and Kiss screamed through the speakers while everyone screamed over the music and rubbed their bodies against each other. In my bedroom, I turned on my portable radio and listened to Peaches & Herb, Michael Jackson, Barry Manilow, or pushed in my favorite red 8-track tape of Sonny & Cher to cancel out the noise on the other side of the door. I swung my hair around and sang along with Cher while coloring or playing with my stuffed animals. I pretended as though nothing abnormal was going on outside of my bedroom door. It was just me doing my own thing, having a softer pop music show for my animals.

This method helped me deal sometimes, but not always.

The parties lasted for hours and eventually, my stomach begged for food. I tried to slip out of my room by staying pressed against the walls, away from everyone else, and slink to the kitchen.

"Hey kiddo," their friend Bill greeted me when he saw me.

I smiled at him, relieved to see he was here. Bill was the nicest one of Jack and Mom's friends. He had a wife and two kids, and always made time to talk to me and ask me how school was going. When my world was constantly filled with drunken strangers taking over our house, coming and going as though they lived there, Bill represented normalcy that I craved. It was nice to see him, although I was surprised he was there when a party was happening. That wasn't normal.

Bill typically stayed at our house when he drove through Salt Lake and needed to crash for the night. He started to come by more often, once or twice a month. Over time, I started noticing slight changes in him.

Even before Bill would knock on the door to enter, I always knew it was him. His shadow crossed the living room window as he approached the door and gave him away. Six-five and skinny, with short black hair, he reminded me of Abraham Lincoln.

Jack, a solid foot shorter than Bill, would encourage Bill to sit down the moment he arrived. He would rush him to a chair, bring him a beer, and start cooking his famous hot dogs with meat sauce. Bill loved those hot dogs as much as we did.

After Bill had stayed with us a few more times, Jack assigned me the task of making sure Bill had everything he needed, drinks and all. I didn't mind, I liked Bill. I would bring him his beer and sit and talk with him. Then he and Jack would start talking about cars or work, Jack cussing his way through his sentences while Bill nodded and laughed. Bill was quiet and always tired. Soon, Jack would shoo my mom off the couch so Bill could lie down and stretch his long body out, his feet dangling awkwardly over the arm of the couch. One of us would get the extra blanket out of the hall closet and since we didn't have an extra pillow, I would have to give mine to Bill.

Then Jack's attention to Bill's needs shifted from sleep and food to something more sinister. "Go sit over by Bill. Look how lonely he is over there by himself. He misses his kids. Go snuggle up with him, Gina. Grab him a drink and grab one of those cute little bottles for you too." Jack rubbed his hands together, plotting whatever gross plan was in his mind.

Bill shifted on the couch, his cheeks red.

Jack often reminded me that he bought cute, pink, mini bottles of wine as though the color would tempt me to join in the drinking games. I hated that he bought those. I wasn't going to drink them. I was mortified that he said it in front of Bill. I doubted Bill bought his kids alcohol.

"I don't want any!" I also didn't want to sit next to Bill. My reserve wasn't because I didn't trust Bill, but I had learned by now how dangerous Jack was.

"Don't you want to be part of the party? You don't want to be the outcast, do you? Go get a bottle for you. I bought them just for you. Gina's drinks. No one else's."

Something within me fluttered. It wasn't doubt or flattery; it was resolve. "No."

Anger flashed in Jack's eyes. He opened his mouth to speak, but Bill cut him off. "You got any trips coming up, Jack?" changing the subject to what Jack liked best: himself.

Once he started talking about himself, it was easier to sneak away. Bill nodded at me as I slipped away to my bedroom, encouraging my departure.

I may have escaped with Bill's help at that time, but Jack was like a dog with a meaty bone; he didn't let up. He remained persistent. Each time Bill was over, he dangled alcohol in front of me as though I might change my mind, and then dangled me in front of Bill like bait. Bill didn't seem like a threat, but Jack could be persuasive.

"Doesn't Gina look good today in the new t-shirt we brought her back from Denver?" Jack asked Bill when I brought them their requested drinks. "Oh, look at how lonesome Bill is over there. Go sit on his lap, Gina."

"No," I said while shoving away the bottle Jack wiggled in front of my eyes.

Jack hated not being able to control people, and his

playful façade melted. "Go take this and go sit on Bill's lap, you fucking brat."

I hesitated, everything in me telling me to run to my room but I was scared Jack would chase after me. He had been drinking for hours. As I stood there, debating what to do, he continued on his rant, "You are the most fucking selfish brat! Why do we have you? You get in the way, you talk back, and you don't fucking care that Bill misses his kids. You're fucking selfish! When are you going to realize the world doesn't revolve around you?"

I looked at Bill, hoping he would come to my rescue again. But Bill no longer blushed when Jack suggested that I sit on his lap. He smiled at me with a crooked grin, a welcoming one, as though it would be okay if I did sit there. I watched his legs spread a little further, like an invitation.

Clearly, there was only one safe place for me, so I backed away like frightened prey into my bedroom fearing the predators may come for me. *Please, God. Keep me safe.* I shut the door, leaning against it. "I'm not selfish," I said under my breath. "I'm not selfish." Again and again, I spoke the words aloud, talking over the reverberating memory of Jack's words. I slid into my pajamas and lay my head on my stuffed bear, tears falling onto his cheek as I drifted off to sleep, praying that God keep Nino and me safe.

Later, I was awoken by a strange noise. Was it the TV? No. Was it an animal? No... not Nino!

I cracked opened my door and listened. Was it my mom? This was a sound I rarely heard. She was crying...no, she was sobbing. Something was wrong.

I crept down the hallway. I was afraid, though I didn't know what I would find.

Goosebumps covered my arms before I saw them.

My mom was lying naked on her back, her feet planted

on the floor, and her legs spread wide. Three naked men lay around her. Polaroids covered the floor, but instead of what I'd seen that day in their dresser drawer, this was happening in real time right before my eyes.

Jack was sitting in his chair with the camera. My mom was on the floor about three feet away from him. I immediately recognized one of the three men.

Bill.

He lay on his side, gazing at my mom while his finger danced around her skin. His slender body only covered by white underwear. The other men looked on while they smoked cigarettes in the nude.

No one cared that my mom was weeping.

Why isn't Bill helping her? She needs help. He has to see that she needs help. She's crying.

When I heard Jack's camera click, I knew the truth.

This was all intentional.

I slipped away without anyone seeing me, leaning on the wall as though it would help hold me up. Back in my room, I lay on my bed as my stomach cramped with fear.

I would never trust Bill again.

Jack, Bill, and all these men were disgusting, evil creatures.

My mom's naked body, exposed. Images I couldn't shake, entering a world I shouldn't have known existed, especially not in our home.

13

AWARENESS

*A*s my body became more defined with its feminine features, Jack's advances were emboldened. More frequent touches that snuck under my clothes. An increase in sexual comments.

Mom was a witness to it all. She continued to ignore them.

I was only a child.

When a child is playing with a ball and it rolls out into the street, the child looks at their parent for a cue as to whether or not it's okay to run out into the street to grab the ball. Children need their parents to provide guidance. But my mom was silent, looking away. She didn't just allow me to chase the ball into the street; she turned her head while the cars were heading straight for me. Danger was always around. She saw it and ignored it every single time.

Mom expressed emotion in the form of anger only when I disappointed Jack or interrupted their time together. Otherwise, she held the same sentiments toward me as I had developed for her: none. There was an expectation for me to respect her; she was my mom after all. That's what Jack told me. That's what the community I lived in told me. Everyone was expected to "Honor thy mother and father."

My dad had remarried and had his hands full between work, his new wife, and her three daughters. He still picked me up on Sundays, but it was a little different now that it wasn't just us. I liked Sherry and her daughters. They were much younger than me at two, five, and eight-years-old, but I enjoyed being with all of them. Sherry was striking with high cheekbones, long auburn hair, and a smile that would stop you in your tracks. Her girls had white hair and reminded me of the bleach blond family. They were well behaved and I felt a bit like a big sister to them. I would be starting junior high school in a few months, and Sherry treated me like the big sister. I felt responsible around her, as if I fit in and could help her by playing with the girls while she cooked dinner or folded laundry. She would ask if I wanted her to paint my nails or braid my hair. I loved all of it! I felt like a part of the family, even if it was only a couple of times per month.

The day I started my period, my mom angrily threw a tampon at me, upset that I had yelled through the bathroom door for help when I noticed unexpected blood. I'm sure she was right in the middle of watching "The Dating Game," and I had interrupted it. I had no idea what was happening to me. Well, maybe a little bit of an idea. Judy Blume's *Are You There God? It's Me, Margaret* had prepared me somewhat for this day. However, I didn't realize I was old enough to start my cycle. At eleven-years-old, I was the same age as Margaret, but I thought my mom or someone would have prepared me for something as important as this. It's one thing to read about it in a book; it's an entirely different thing when it happens to you. It's funny to think about that now. Even though there had been no evidence of mothering from her, as a child I still expected it. It would be years before I admitted it to myself and even more years before I accepted that Mom was simply not going to pick up that responsibility.

The following month, I was at my dad and Sherry's house when my period came again. Hanging my head, I told Sherry what was happening and that my mom had given me a tampon last month, but I was afraid to use it. I had been wadding toilet paper up and sticking it between myself and my underwear. Sherry wrapped me in a big hug, took me into her bathroom and showed me how to use a pad. She laughed and said, "This being a woman thing is tough enough, you should at least be as comfortable as possible! These will help." Later that evening, she went to the store and bought a box of pads that she stored in the cabinet of the spare bathroom for me. She also snuck a box into my overnight bag.

I had a new family and a new house at my dad's, and after years of living at the King's Row apartments, I moved with Jack and Mom to a duplex in Magna. Magna was even farther from Bountiful, my true home. Now I had a new school, too. There were a lot of changes all at once.

From the moment we pulled up and saw the chipped white paint of the Magna duplex, it was as though a permanent cloud resided over the place, darkening the sky, sending a bitter chill in the air. The sun could have been shining every day, but it didn't feel like it in Magna.

The people who lived in the other side of the duplex watched us move in, not saying a word, just staring at us. Two older teenaged boys sat on their front porch, one of them not taking his eyes off me, a look reminiscent of Jack's eyes when things were about to take a turn.

I didn't like this place. Not at all. My bedroom was at the front of the house, right off the living room. The window hung above the front porch. That same porch connected to the place those creepy boys were sitting. I shuddered when I realized how close they were to my new room. I rushed to make sure the window in my room locked tightly. Thank God it did. There was only one bathroom that I had to share with my mom and Jack.

The home sat alone on a busy main street with a fire station directly across from it. Cars were constantly zooming by, and the trucks' sirens blasted through the air making me jump straight out of my bed many nights. Our only neighbors creeped me out and were connected to us by only a shared wall and driveway, a bit too close for comfort.

There were a washer and dryer but no swimming pool. I wondered if Jack would be bored without his weekly laundry and pool shenanigans.

Without the rotation of neighbors at King's Row to watch me, Mom and Jack were forced to drag me along on more of their long-haul trips.

I would sit in the bed area of the semi while Mom and Jack sat up front. NPR was always on the radio. I did word searches and colored to pass the time, holding my bladder so I wouldn't have to ask them to stop to use the bathroom. They were already miserable that I was with them.

With three of us in the truck, there wasn't enough room to sleep in the truck bed. We had to stay at motels, which pissed Jack off. He was forced to spend money because "the brat is with us."

On one of the first few trips that summer, we pulled over

to stay in a motel. The long walkways were similar to that of my dad's old apartment. As we walked to our room, Jack grumbled about how much I was always costing him money. We entered our room and threw our bags down. Jack immediately grabbed the Black Velvet and poured two drinks, one for him and one for Mom.

I yawned. It was late, and after traveling for most of the day, I was ready for bed.

Jack watched me as I changed into pajamas. I didn't think anything about it. I was used to his eyes on me.

He picked up the empty ice container and threw it at Mom. "Go get some ice," he demanded, not taking his eyes off me while sipping his drink.

She slipped out the door without a word, shutting it tightly behind her.

Jack peeked out the window to make sure Mom was gone, then turned to me. "Lay on the bed."

I was planning on doing just that so I could go to sleep, but the unsettling way he spoke the words made the hair on the back of my neck stand up. I crawled onto the thin comforter.

Jack pulled his camera out of the bag.

I hated that camera. I held my breath as I waited for the click.

He snapped the button on it, a picture slid out, and he shook it until it came into focus. He held it in front of his face and evaluated it with a grin. "I like you in those pajamas."

Jack set his camera down on the table, and I exhaled with relief. Only one picture tonight. Good.

But he wasn't done. "I'd like you even more without them. Take them off."

I froze, watching the door, waiting for my mom to come back in.

"What did I tell you to do, Gina?"

I spoke slowly, "Take my pajamas off."

Jack's eyebrows arched as he nodded.

This was new.

I bit my inner cheek, fighting the urge to scream as my clothes slid off, the scratchiness of the comforter nipping at my bare body.

I did as I was told because I was scared of him, especially when he was drinking. I also knew my mom would be right back; she just went to get ice. He was just going to take some pictures and when she got back, he would turn his attention back to her. That's what I thought because that is what always happened.

But this time she didn't come back.

Click. The camera. The chill in the air had me shaking. At least being photographed before, I always had one of those stupid teddies or nightgowns on. This time, everything was exposed.

Jack only took one more picture, shaking it into focus with a smirk. He slid the photo and the camera back in the bag.

It's over with. It's done. Whew.

But instead of allowing me to put my clothes back on, Jack walked toward me. He spoke of special kisses, concepts I couldn't understand. Fear consumed me, clouding my vision, clogging my ears, and all I could think about was whether or not I had the correct reaction on my face. I didn't know what Jack was talking about, but if I didn't react right, his anger would be worse.

As he leaned over me, he began to pull my legs apart.

My mom, the Polaroids, the parties. All of the horrific memories came rushing back.

Oh God, please send her back here. What is happening?

My knuckles whitened as I clenched the bedspread. Terror ran through my body like a raging river. Tears streamed down my face. Jack didn't see them. Or maybe he didn't care.

I had been used to Jack's ongoing touches and advances, numbing myself when necessary, but this was different. My mind was spinning, trying to process and reject it all at once.

My eyes kept cutting to the door, pleading for my mom to walk in. Surely he would stop when she walked in. He had to stop.

Where is Mom? Oh, God, please send her back. Even she would know this was wrong.

I held my breath, focusing on the noise of the ice machine. It couldn't be that far away. This was a small motel. She would be back soon. *Where in the world could she have gone?*

But time passed, and the door stayed closed.

This isn't right. This definitely isn't right.

This is a movie. This is not really happening. This is not happening to me.

I wanted to throw up. I tried to still my body. Like playing dead. Maybe he'd stop.

But Jack didn't care.

A trip to get ice should have taken minutes, but Mom was gone for far longer.

By the time Mom finally returned, my pajamas were back on. I hid under the covers—my stomach churning loudly, my body still trembling—pretending I was asleep.

Jack was sitting on a chair, watching TV with a drink in his hand.

He didn't question her. He didn't ask why it took her so damn long to get ice from a machine that was just down the walkway. He would have normally.

Does she know? Did she leave on purpose so Jack could do what he just did to me?

I couldn't allow myself to believe it. Why would a mother let that happen to her daughter? Doesn't she think I'm worth protecting?

I am. I know I am!

Mom's actions spoke louder than words ever could. Jack made it clear that all women would end up naked on magazines or as prostitutes someday, and my mom clearly believed her daughter's worth amounted to the same.

Back at the creepy duplex, Jack would frequently come into my room or into the shared bathroom while I was taking a bath, replicating the motel scene. I was easy prey.

Where is my mom? I wondered over and over again. Her allowing him to touch me was one thing, but this was something else entirely. She was always in the house. They never left each other, yet when he disappeared to find me, she never came looking for him.

The questions grew in desperation each time Jack repeated the act, helping himself to me anytime he wanted. You may wonder why I didn't fight him off or tell him no. These advances, along with Jack's anger, came in small bits throughout a long period of my childhood. This is what molesters do. By the time they get to this point, we, the abused, are operating like robots. Couple that with my mom, someone who should have protected me, yet allowed it to happen, the confusion and shock is paralyzing to a child.

The moment I realized she was purposefully leaving me alone with him was the moment I began to shake myself out of my frozen state. I became wholly aware of my plight. Twelve-years-old and the last of perceived childhood security was stripped away.

I've often wondered if child molesters and their accomplices consider the fact that the children they are abusing will grow up.

14

THE PARAKEET DRAWING

I had fully realized by now I wasn't safe with my mom and Jack with their friends. I stayed on high alert at all times. The parties had decreased in frequency, but Jack and his friends had increased in danger.

The groups filtering in often came straight from the bars, so they were already several drinks in. The house got loud and full of random bodies quickly. None of them cared that the second bedroom belonged to a little girl. Soon there were couples on my bed groping each other. I would slide out of the closet door and run to hide in the bathroom, jumping in the tub and pulling the shower curtain shut to hide. Soon that was taken over, too. Sex on the counter or vomiting up their pills and drinks in the toilet.

One night, with nowhere to go, I clutched my coloring books and crayons close to my chest as I ran through the haze of cigarette smoke to the only safe place left. Mom's precious living room table, protected with that long table-cloth draped over it. It was the last hiding spot where I could block out the sexual groans, snorting of drugs, or dry heaves. I didn't like the rock music, cursing, or crude jokes that existed out in the living room, but it was much better than the other stuff.

Bottles and drinks layered the table as alcohol dripped down the sides and stained the fabric. I knew my mom would be pissed about those later when she sobered up. The table, an item she showed more care for than she ever did for her daughter, was a temporary haven for me. I was in the middle of the chaos, but no one knew I was there. Once I realized this, it became my go-to spot every time before a party started. It worked several times. Several times I was alone. Safe.

Another party was starting, so I immediately slid beneath the tablecloth and positioned myself in my spot. Situating my books on the carpet, I focused on coloring within the lines of each picture. For hours I did this, blocking out the music and drunk strangers, happily coloring away, lost in my own world.

Suddenly to my left, the tablecloth jerked up and away from the floor. A man I had never seen before peeked his head underneath.

"Hello," he said with a grin, his head cocked sideways.

I froze. Terrified. The coloring book slipped from my lap while I clutched the black crayon in my hand.

Now what? Where do I go? Do I run? Am I safer in here or out there with them?

I wondered if he could hear my heart beating against my chest.

If I screamed, no one would come to my rescue. They were too drunk. The music was too loud.

I'd been in this world long enough to see that no one cared about the little girl in the middle of an alcohol-drug-and-sex-infused party. If they did, I wouldn't be hiding under the table in the first place.

"What are you doing under here?" the man asked.

I kept my mouth closed. I was still processing my escape.

"Can I come in there with you?"

Does it matter what I say? It doesn't. I already know that. This is a trick. He wants me to think I have a choice so I will trust him. That's what adults do. Trick me.

He didn't wait for my answer. He crouched on his hands and knees, and crawled under the table next to me letting the tablecloth drop behind him and close us in.

"It's okay," he tried to comfort me, but I had heard those words from Jack too many times to relax. "Can you show me what you're coloring?"

I figured Jack saw me hide here and sent this man under the tablecloth. This man must be like the new Bill to Jack.

I shifted from the man, far enough away that my shoulder wasn't touching him yet not too far away that my other shoulder would peek out from the tablecloth. If that happened, people would know I was under here. Hiding with a strange man and being seen by the drunk partygoers both seemed dangerous in their own right. I couldn't figure out which one was worse.

I kept my eyes directed on the floor as I plotted an escape. If this man would make a sudden move, I was sure I could lift the tablecloth and dart out. I would probably run into someone's leg and that could cause a disruption. I didn't want to be the reason for a scene to be caused. Jack would not like that at all.

I picked up the coloring book, still not looking at the stranger, and flipped through the pages I had done so far, apprehensive about why he was under here. I had learned there were very few men I could trust. Very few indeed. My dad, and that was it. This wasn't my dad.

"That's really good coloring. Do you like to draw?"

My mind rushed to Jack's mice game. This man was going to ask me to take off my shirt so he could draw mice on my chest. I knew how this worked.

I shook my head, even though that wasn't true.

"Drawing is one of my favorite things to do. I saw you have a parakeet. What's his name?"

"Nino," I whispered.

"Nino." He smiled. "That's a good name for a bird."

It is? "My mom said it was a fucking stupid name."

The man took the crayon out of my hand, and I tensed as his hand brushed mine. He put it to a blank sheet of paper and started drawing the curve of a parakeet's beak, followed by the head, body, and feathers.

"Does that look like Nino?"

I shook my head with a giggle, still not making any eye contact with him, ready to flee at any moment. It looked like a fluffy Nino, a cartoon version of him, but I loved it.

"Want me to teach you how to draw it?"

"Yes, please." I whispered, eyes down, hands shaking.

The man drew it again, but slowly this time, explaining each line and how to connect them to form the picture. Then he handed the crayon back to me and instructed me how to do it. I furrowed my brow in concentration as I glanced at the one he did while listening to his direction.

After a few tries, I finally got it.

"Wow, that's a great bird! That may be better than mine!"

I beamed at him. "I could hang it up by Nino's cage like it's a little friend for him."

I caught myself quickly. *Don't trust him!*

I looked back down at the floor and away from him. *Is my escape still possible? Anyone standing there, blocking the way?*

"I'm sure Nino would love that. You should try drawing another one in color this time. What color do you want to make him?"

I opted for blue in honor of Pat.

The man clapped as my colored parakeet was complete. "That's great. You're a fast learner! Draw another one, this time green with yellow."

Then another. "Let's draw Pat again and add purple to the blue."

"Draw another one and you pick the color this time."

We sat under the table drawing parakeets for over an hour. I was having more fun than I had had in years.

The man said he had to go. He picked up all the drawings of the birds and stacked them neatly together, handing them to me. I took them and finally looked up at him, meeting his eyes before quickly looking back down at the floor. I was surprised by the disappointment that struck me. I didn't want him to go. Not just because I was having fun, but because he brought me peace. More peace than I had ever known. For the first time in years, I was calm. My insides were screaming, "Don't leave. I'm scared. I'm not safe here."

He maneuvered himself around in the small space, getting up on his hands and knees before lifting the tablecloth and backing out from under the table. Just before his head disappeared, he turned to me one more time, his face shadowed by the cloth and only a few inches away from mine. I finally felt bold enough to lift my head and look at him directly. I needed to look at his eyes; maybe he would see how scared I was in this house.

He spoke slowly, "Listen to me. Everything will be okay. Just keep drawing the parakeet, okay?"

I nodded, his words catching me off guard.

He smiled. "If anything is ever troubling you, if you are worried or scared, draw the parakeet. You are going to be okay."

Then he was gone, the tablecloth swaying from his last touch.

Everything will be okay.

I kept drawing new versions of the parakeet, carefully trying variations of greens and blues while the party continued on around me.

As the crayon scratched against the paper, I thought about how Jack and Mom had no clue where I was. Jack didn't send him in. The man found me on his own. He saw me. He didn't want anything in return. He only wanted to be kind to the forgotten girl hiding under a table.

When I didn't draw the parakeet right the first time, the man didn't give up on me. He kept encouraging me, having faith that I would get it. He was patient with me and cheered me on.

And then he left without anything given to him in return.

I began to realize the world did not have to be as dark as it had been. I would be okay. I didn't know how, but suddenly I had hope to cling to. I had this drawing and the peace that came from it.

Everything in the last five years had been for survival, but it was going to be okay. *I was going to be okay.*

I took a deep breath and suddenly felt a little lighter. Nothing would be the same again.

PICTURES

Gina at age 5 with her mom and dad.

Gina's school picture at age 9 after returning from Grandma Walker's summer of grilled cheese.

Gina, around age 11 - This picture was found when Gina was researching the book. She was surprised to look at this picture and not recognize the girl in the photo. It was sad evidence of those blocks of time in her memory. This would have been at the height of the parties and molestation.

Gina at age 12 dressed up in an outfit Jack bought her for the house parties in Magna.

Gina at age 15, a year after moving in with her dad.

Gina with her dad the day of her high school graduation.

Gina, age 18, at basic training waiting to call her Dad.

PART II

15

FLEEING THE DARKNESS

The parakeet drawing didn't magically change things, but it was the start of the transition to the strength rising within. Such a simple cartoonish image instilled a hope that rooted itself in my soul. Maybe it was knowing that the man had every chance to do something bad to me. He could have gotten away with it. When sex, drugs, and alcohol were dripping off the walls and from everyone in the room, he chose to spend an hour with a child, teaching me how to draw a figure of comfort.

I sat in my room, in the bed of Jack's truck, in the car, in the living room, in school drawing the parakeet.

Sometimes I drew it without consciously realizing it.

It was a symbol of light within the dark. Comfort when I needed it the most.

The reminder that everything will be okay.

The reminder that good existed.

My mom continued to live life as though I was not there. The molestation didn't stop.

Yet, the parakeet drawing brought light into my world.

Things would change someday. I would be free. I knew it.

It was clear I was going to have to take care of myself, though.

Over the next year, my body rapidly changed shape. My breasts formed, becoming more representative of my mom's, a fact I despised. Between those and my hips, an hourglass figure resulted. I was growing. No longer a child, not yet a woman.

Jack and Mom were pushing me more and more toward the mini bottles they bought "especially for me." More and more toward the men who came to dinner. More and more toward the couples at the parties. Alcohol. Drugs. Sex. Their world.

But I didn't want it. I had seen what those things resulted in. I had no desire to be like them.

After finally being caught hiding out under the table at the last party, I was now forced to keep my bedroom door open where Jack could see me on the days they threw a party. I was forced to be "at" it, even if that was by sitting in my room alone. Jack made sure I didn't stay alone, though. He brought a man in to sit with me on my bed, handing me a drink and telling me to smile and visit with whatever his name was.

I knew I would get hurt more if I stayed here. There was no question.

That was it. *I'm not doing this anymore.*

From the moment my eyes snapped opened in the morning, my senses were called to stand alert. Later in life, I could relate it to living in a war zone. Each moment I was awake, adrenaline was running through my veins. High alert, ready, clarity to hide, run or save myself in some way.

Always thinking about the worst-case scenario and preparing myself to handle it.

Where is Jack?

Where is my mom?

Who's in the house?

How are you going to get out of here?

How are you going to protect yourself?

Don't think. Do that. Go.

It started with saying no.

I began to tell Jack no.

When I did, he didn't force anything.

He didn't like it. He called me a fucking wop, a fucking brat, many of the same words he had used in the past to degrade me.

But when I said no, he knew I meant it.

It was such a simple word, and I liked it. My one word overpowered his degrading insults. They didn't affect me like they once did, no matter what phrases he slung at me.

The next time my dad picked me up, I told him, "I want to live with you." We were driving back to his house from Magna at the time. I'll never forget the look on his face when he turned his head, looked straight at me and said, "okay."

Just like that, it was "okay."

I was shocked.

Relieved.

Excited.

Confused.

If it was that easy, why hadn't it happened before now?

Should I have asked him sooner?

Why hadn't he offered it himself?

And then I thought—who cares, I am going to be safe.

Pure relief settled into my bones, and I no longer cared about anything but that peace and safety.

The summer between seventh and eighth grades, I took Nino and moved in with my dad.

Dad and Sherry's marriage had not lasted long. He was on his own for a bit before rekindling a romance with his high school sweetheart, Ike. She was a cashier at Safeway at the time, and he was on a worksite and had run into the store to grab something for lunch. Once he saw her, he snuck into her line to say hello. Ike was beautiful, fare-skinned, luscious dark brown hair, high eyebrows and a captivating smile. She was slim and dressed nice, always donning the newest styles. The best part was her fun and teasing demeanor. Everyone, not just the men, wanted to go through her aisle to check out. She would tease and laugh, ask how their kids were doing or how that new job was coming along. It was easy to see why she caught Dad's eye again. She made him happy, which he deserved.

Dad had just moved in with Ike and her three kids. I thought it was perfect and meant to be that I fit right in between Kim, who was fifteen and Jason, age eleven, with Lisa the youngest at ten-years-old. The house they lived in was a warm welcome from the dark Magna duplex Jack and Mom lived in. A tiny brick house tucked away in a suburban neighborhood with a clean and bright vibe. The neighborhood was full of kids and teenagers, families who had lived there and taken care of one another for years. There was even a bonus—the neighbor across the street had horses in their backyard!

Best of all, it felt safe.

The chaos wasn't much less, but it was a different kind of chaos. No one was touching me. The walls weren't pumping out rock music and there weren't parties filled with strangers having sex in my bedroom.

It just wasn't the joyful life I imagined of other families living either.

But I was safe. I reminded myself this constantly.

Dad and Ike came home every night at the expected time. We had a dog and a cat to keep Nino and me company. There was always food in the fridge. Even though he was working a lot, I got to be around my dad more, and I loved that. My dad was still my hero.

I was stuck in a mode of watching everything unroll like a movie. That had been my default for so long that it was hard to snap out of it. No one in Ike's household had any idea that I had just walked out of a war zone and was cautiously feeling my way through this new environment. They had no idea I was on high alert at all times, treading lightly in case there were land mines here like the ones at my Mom and Jack's.

There were.

These landmines were different.

Ike was going through a tough time as Kim, her oldest daughter, had just been in a horrific accident. Ike's stress level was clearly present each day as she tried to help Kim heal both physically and emotionally. Now she was taking on Dad's daughter in an already full household.

Ike expected a clean house and for the kids to fill the role. She worked long hours and needed the help. Now, she had a new cleaner. Her kids were glad I was there to do it, too. It seemed to be the only thing they were pleased about with my arrival.

I didn't know if the pandemonium had always been there or if it was a result of dad and I moving in, but the walls shrunk in a short amount of time. The conflicts, the yelling, and the constant tension were bursting the joints of the house.

A prime example of the chaos was the Sloppy Joe Fiasco Heard Around the World of 1981.

Ike spent the evening cooking up the sloppiest of sloppy joes. When they were ready, everyone gathered around the table for a pleasant family dinner. Except as she delivered plates of messy sandwiches to each of us, she was exchanging not-uncommon-unpleasantries with her daughter.

"Fuck off!" Kim suddenly screeched. She picked up her hot sloppy joe and threw it in Ike's face.

"Don't you do that to your mom!" My dad pushed his chair back and hastily stood up.

The yelling exploded from all sides of the table. Ike cursed while wiping chunky meat sauce off her face. Everyone was fired up. It sounded like ten different topics were being argued about at once, and I couldn't decipher any of them.

My heart raced. My stomach knotted. Fear rose within me. I stayed silent in my chair. My hand twitched as I wished I had a pencil so I could draw the parakeet to calm down.

Inside, I was begging for the kids to be more controlled. For the fights to diminish. For people to stop yelling. I wanted to run away. *I can't be around this. Bad things happen when there's this much anger.*

Ike and her kids seemed to really struggle. It was hard for me to understand. I didn't think the things she asked of them were too much to expect. Her desire to parent and control them while dealing with the undercurrents of her divorce and Kim's newfound pain was like a match waiting to be lit. Something as innocent as sitting around the dining room table could be dangerous, a family moment I craved for years turned frightening and opened up my fight or flight response within moments.

Luckily, I could go to my room, spend time with my dad, Nino, or Sam the cat to ease the anxiety. I could go on walks or ride my bike. I was always a little nervous, afraid I was doing something wrong. I didn't know what this life was supposed to look like. I was hopeful of a better world, and I wanted to do the right things—the things that would make my dad, and Ike, happy.

At school, I was becoming a new person. Actually, I was building confidence and blooming into my true self. My happiness shone, and it came through as I made friends with everyone. The cheerleaders, the athletes, the stoners, the geeks, the "gangs," even the few groups of people of color—further proof I was breaking away from Jack's control. I was a source for guys to learn about girls they wanted to date and a peacemaker for those who were not getting along. My experiences in life had matured me faster than I'd wish on anyone my age. I thought about the bigger picture at all times, understanding that moments—good and bad—are fleeting. Everything was temporary. But I also had hope more than ever before about the future.

Back at home, I was quieter. I did as I was told, working to win over love and affection. I worked hard to stay within the lines Ike set, especially since her kids weren't doing so. I cleaned. I cooked because Ike didn't have time to, and frankly didn't want to. Most days I enjoyed doing it because I wanted Dad to have good meals since he worked so hard and loved food so much.

I made recipes found in various cookbooks, like a beef stroganoff casserole that looked delicious. The first time I made it for dinner, everyone liked it and said how good it was. I was super proud that they liked it! So, I made it three days in a row. If everyone enjoyed it, why break what's working? I was desperate to hold on to the good things.

Ike wrinkled her nose on day three. "Is that all you can make? I think you need to try something new. There is a tuna casserole recipe that everyone likes, why don't you try that one tomorrow?"

The kids jumped right in on it, "Yeah, is that all you can make?"

It became a running joke.

"What's for dinner tonight, Gina? Shit on a shingle again?" They laughed and sneered.

I thought I was making them happy, but it was short-lived. Nobody else was cooking, and now that Ike suggested the tuna casserole, it looked like I was going to be doing more of it.

I wanted to be liked, I wanted to help out, but everything I was doing didn't seem to be enough. I didn't mind doing my part, but my part soon became doing my tasks and Kim's. Ike did not want to upset Kim more, and Kim held a lot of anger from her accident. Rightfully so after what she had been through. Still, I was walking out of my own personal hell, and all I wanted was peace. If that meant I did more cleaning and all the cooking. So be it.

Over the next few years, Dad added onto the house. He built a shop out back and finished the basement so we had more bedrooms and a family room. Many of my weekends were spent holding up sheetrock as he nailed it to the beams that would form a new room, or painting the baseboards while he painted the walls.

All of us kids took turns with driving lessons in Ike's olive green 1974 Mustang. First Kim learned how to drive in it, then me. We each added a few scratches and dings to Ike's baby. Eventually I wanted my own car. I had a part-time job and could afford a $50 per month car payment.

My dad helped me look for cars for months. I found a dream car. I was set on it. He was not. It was a navy blue 1971 Fiat Spider convertible. I was a high school junior, sixteen-years-old, and in love with that car. He was adamant that buying this car was not a good idea! Then, Nino died. Dad relented and loaned me the money, ensuring I signed a contract with him agreeing to pay him back $50 per month.

Everyone knew how much I loved Nino, but they had no idea why. They had teased me about my attachment to him until he died. Then they were concerned about me. I didn't have much emotion when he passed away. Inside I was so grateful I had had him for nine years. I knew he had been there for me when I needed him the most. I felt safe now. It felt like a little more of my life with my mom and Jack died when Nino died. Ike and her kids tiptoed around me for days unsure why I wasn't crying, mourning, or moping around. I was mourning in my own way, by sketching out the parakeet drawing.

One of the benefits about living in this home was that Ike parented her kids, and my dad parented me. They tried to stay out of the way of each other's parenting decisions, so Ike didn't say anything when I was given permission to get my new baby. I loved that car!

For about six months.

Until the block cracked.

I tried to tell you. I knew that was what my Dad was thinking, but he didn't let the words slide out of his mouth. He simply raised his eyebrows, gave me a big hug and said, "It's more important to buy dependable cars than ones that look nice. It was fun while it lasted!"

On the first of the following month, Dad brought his

ledger out to me and asked when he could expect the payment.

"Payment? For the Fiat?"

He nodded.

I wondered if he was losing his memory. "Dad...the Fiat died, remember? Why would I pay you for something that's gone?"

"Because we had an agreement. It doesn't matter if the car is gone or not. I lent you the money and you agreed to pay it back."

He was right. *Damnit!* Integrity of his word, and I had to respect that. At least Dad could be counted on when he spoke.

As the years went on, cleaning the kitchen became my job. That included keeping the kitchen sink clean by drying it out when it was wet. I couldn't help it if other people used the sink afterward. But if it was wet, Ike hated it. Jason would get a drink and splash water all over as he heard his mom coming down the hallway. Then he would slyly walk to the other side of the room and laugh as Ike yelled for me to get in the kitchen and dry the sink out.

Her other pet peeve was the dishwasher. In the 80's the dishwashers were not that great! If you didn't completely wash every bit of food off the dishes before putting them in the dishwasher, you would end up with bits of food baked onto the glasses and silverware. I hated emptying the dishwasher because Ike would inspect those dishes for every little spot and crumb.

"Clean the kitchen, Gina."

"Why is the sink wet, again, Gina?"

"You cook tonight, Gina."

"Empty the dishwasher, Gina."

Cinderella, Cinderella.

Ike worked most evenings as a cashier. If I hadn't done my job right, she would ensure I knew it in the morning.

She wasn't always wrong. Sometimes I took shortcuts. I was a teenager after all. Once, she charged into my room at two in the morning, demanding that I come upstairs with her. Every dish in the house was stacked on the countertops, even those from the China cabinet. "Wash all of these! All of them!" she screamed.

I yawned, wondering if I heard her right or if I was sleeping. "They're clean. Why would I need to wash them?"

"Everything you put away was dirty! If you can't use the dishwasher right, you will clean all these by hand! I will wake you up every time this happens!"

If she demanded that of her kids, they'd throw a glass at her.

All the yelling was starting to take a toll on me. I was farther away from the warzone that existed at Jack and Mom's, but I was also more sure of my footing and my ability to survive in various circumstances.

While Dad and Ike did not get into each other's parenting, he expected me to follow Ike's rules. He had no idea how frustrated I was by the difference in the expectations put on me compared to her kids. They all came and went as they wanted, while I had to be home cleaning and cooking if I wasn't at school or work. I was doing well in school and excited about my upcoming graduation. I had a goal to make my dad proud and finish out school with a decent GPA. But I was tired of coming home to a place that I couldn't focus on school, or even be a kid.

I learned not to invite friends over to my house while living with Jack and Mom, but I was getting more felt comfortable in my new house. After all, Kim, Jason, and Lisa all had friends in the neighborhood who came over all the time. So I finally jumped in and invited my friend Janet over to do homework together.

Within minutes of us starting on our project, Ike swung my bedroom door open, "Go fold the laundry."

I nodded to the books in front of us. "But we're doing homework."

"Go! Laundry!" Turning to Janet, her voice sweetened. "Janet, it was nice seeing you, sweetie, but Gina has chores to do. Time for you to go home."

I winced at her tone, feeling the embarrassment heat my cheeks.

Janet raised an eyebrow at me. "I guess I have to go?"

I shrugged coolly, "I guess so."

It was the last time I invited a friend over. I had learned my lesson, just like before.

I refused to let this keep happening.

"Gina! Go vacuum!" Ike called out again.

This time, I snapped back. Years of feeling unappreciated rose to the surface. "You can't boss me around all the time. Homework is more important that all the cleaning you make you do! You are such a bitch!"

Ike locked me out of the house.

I sat on the patio, waiting, wondering how long she would keep me outside.

As soon as my dad pulled into the driveway, I ran to him, "Dad! She locked me out of the house!"

He shut the truck door with a tired sigh. "What happened?"

"Ike made Janet go home. We were doing homework together for a project we have. Ike always makes me clean and the one time I have a friend over, she made her leave! She is such a bitch!" I recounted what happened as though it wasn't a big deal. I spent years not telling Dad how I truly felt about my life and that got me nowhere. Now he needed to know what I was going through.

Dad's eyes widened in a way I had only seen once before in my life. My dad, who had never spanked me, was staring at me with pure fury, nostrils flaring, veins in his neck protruding. Flight mode kicked in, and I started running, equally surprised and scared when Dad chased after me, quicker than I thought he could run. He reached out and grabbed my long hair, pulling me back. He pushed me against the brick house like he had done with Jack years earlier. "Don't you ever call her that again. Do you hear me?"

I nodded, too shocked to say more. Dad let go, exhaustion replacing the anger in his eyes. He used his key to enter the house, not looking back at me.

My breath had escaped me. My blood was pumping. I wasn't scared that he would hurt me because I knew he wouldn't, but I had never seen him so mad at me.

I lost my only advocate in the house. Dad wouldn't tell Ike to stop treating me like a workhorse now that I called her a bitch. I was on my own.

I was angry at the injustice. I wanted my dad to be happy and I knew he loved Ike and me. He was tired. He worked hard and was dealing with the things that come with combining families. That said, he had a life that he chose. I also wanted to choose a life for myself. This was not it. I wanted to do well in school. I wanted to graduate with a decent GPA. I simply wanted to do my homework and share the chores that needed to be done. I had to stand up for what I thought was important for my life. I believed it, and I was not going to back down. I repeated the promise I made to myself when I was with Jack and Mom. *I'm going take care of myself.*

Graduation. I had to stay focused on graduation, my hope for a better future. I was seventeen-years-old. I wasn't going to live here anymore, and there was only one other place to go.

So I went back to where I could at least find silence and solitude: Jack and Mom's.

16

GOING AT IT ALONE

*L*iving with Jack and Mom was different this time.

I kept to myself, away from them. If they were home, I was gone, only coming back later that night so I could sleep.

I existed, that was it. I didn't have to participate in life with them. I got up, got dressed, and went to school. Graduation was my sole focus. I kept my head down and did what I needed to do to get out as soon as possible. I didn't have to depend on them for anything, except for a place to sleep.

No sense in expecting anything from them. I learned early I would only be met with disappointments. I could now play by my own rules. I was simply a roommate, not their child.

This wasn't always clear to Jack who still tried to own me, though.

"Jack is mad at you," Mom commented as she breezed by me in the kitchen.

I took a bite of an apple, not terribly surprised that Jack was pissed at something again. "What'd I do?"

"He doesn't understand why you lock the bathroom door when you shower. He hates that."

There would be only one way that Jack could know that my bathroom door was locked when I showered. He would have had to test the handle.

"Oh?" I threw the apple in the trash and walked away from her, disgusted that she would even think that was worth communicating to me. Did she think that I might actually unlock the door and allow him to defile me, again?

I continued to lock the bathroom door. Every single time.

Jack no longer had control over me.

And he hated it.

I graduated from high school and celebrated with my Dad. My mom didn't come to it, neither did Jack.

After all that work to get here, now I wasn't sure what to do next.

Graduation happened a month before I turned eighteen-years-old. Two options were given to me: live with my mom or dad until I was eighteen, but then I had to pay rent or move out.

I wasn't going to pay rent to be miserable in either one of their houses. If I had to pay, I would live somewhere I wanted to be.

Kim was in search of the same next step since she had graduated as well, so we decided to get an apartment together. We were broke and needed to split the rent on the cheapest place we could find. The result was an upstairs apartment in one of the worst areas we could live in Salt Lake. More reminiscent of a seedy motel than a house, but we were finally independent from our parents. We didn't get along in Ike's house, but our quest for freedom brought us together here.

Back when I was in eighth grade, I had announced my first crush on a boy. I was already navigating the other difficulties of being a teenager while being more wounded than I knew at the time, so I shared it with my mom, thinking it may help us bond.

"What color is he?" Mom had asked. Just like Jack.

"Oh, ahhh.... brown."

Why didn't I think about this before I said anything? I should have known my attempt at bonding wouldn't get us anywhere.

Truth is, the sweet brown-skinned young men were all I had ever been attracted to. They said kind words flattering me that was not the same language that the vulgar white boys used. I had seen white boys grow up to be men that I did not want anything to do with. Jack. Bill. The other nameless men who gang raped my mom for fun. Apart from my dad, the majority of white men were overwhelmingly terrifying.

The first time I saw a black man was when I opened up the apartment door at King's Row and met Henry, Octavia's sweet and gentle husband. The second time was when Kim and I went to the park. I was instantly attracted to a group of men playing basketball, but Randy stuck out the most.

Randy was in the Air Force, stationed at Hill Air Force Base (AFB). He was twenty-six and I was eighteen when we started dating. I didn't know what I was doing or how to properly date, but he was such a gentleman. He would pick me up in his Mazda RX-7 that reminded me of my Fiat, although much nicer! We hung out at his apartment, and I made dinner for him and his roommate.

Was this dating? I couldn't say. I had only begun to have girlfriends to talk to about these things, slowly crawling out of my safe bubble where people couldn't discover more about my life. Mom definitely didn't prepare me for anything. I didn't know what was normal and what wasn't.

Randy knew what was normal, and he was pushing for a more serious relationship. He was ready to settle down. Marriage. Kids. The full home life.

However, I was only getting started in exploring this new world, and that wasn't yet on my mind.

The scars in my life were becoming more visible as I branched out on my own.

If I were out with friends and a fight broke out, I immediately wanted to leave. If they wouldn't leave, I would walk home from wherever I was. *Go. Flee. Get out before something happens to you.* It's hard to break some automatic responses. My entire life had been a battle of the question, how do I protect myself? Where am I going to be safe?

If I was around people making bad decisions, I'd put up walls or sever the relationship. It all related back to Jack and Mom. Their terrible decisions damaged me and stripped away my childhood. I learned to hold the goodness inside closer, not letting just anyone have access to it for fear that they'd take it, too.

Rock music sent panic through my veins. It was too reminiscent of the parties and the men who were at them, so when I was introduced to dance music, it freed part of my spirit.

Xenon, the Utah version of a member-exclusive club for eighteen- to twenty-one-year-olds, captured my attention with the bright lights and energetic dance music. When a friend told me about it and asked me to come along, I was nervous, but deep inside the innate pull to it told me I would be here often.

The excitement pulsated off the walls as soon as we stepped through the entrance door and walked down the dark hallway to enter the great room. The dance floor sat in the center of the room, elevated like a boxing ring. The only way to it was by walking up the stairs. From that view, the entire bar and everyone there was in sight.

A man invited me to dance. I accepted, gliding up the stairs and onto the dance floor. With a deep breath, I allowed myself to enter a place of vulnerability among strangers and let go of control, the music moving my body, losing myself in the electric atmosphere.

It was official: I loved to dance. I didn't know it until that moment. It shouldn't come as a shock. Nino loved dancing, too. It was in me. Hours passed and I wouldn't stop dancing. We spent nearly every weekend there that summer. I looked forward to it all week, counting down the days, then the hours. I was making new friends and once in a while, Randy joined me. He didn't like to dance and had a preference to be down the street at his over-twenty-one club. That was okay with me. There were plenty of people to dance with, especially a few Black and Pacific Island men who I especially enjoyed talking to. I was wrapped in comfort here. This was my place.

The best night happened toward the end of summer. I was dancing at the front of the dance floor, on a high in my element. When the song stopped, I turned around to face a piece of Heaven. The room was full of men I had never seen before. They were smiling up at me—and, yes, I was smiling back. The University of Utah's football team's first night out after weeks of football camp.

I stepped down from the dancing rink to get a drink, and one of the players, Curtis, approached me. We immediately hit it off. "Want to go out some time?" he asked before they left.

"Absolutely."

I went from never dating to now having two men in my life. Curtis was from California and was a lot of fun, always making me laugh. Randy, however, was quiet, stable, and dependable.

If there was a time to choose one of them, I didn't. Instead, I discovered other plans waiting for me.

As MUCH OF an escape as Xenon provided, it wasn't enough.

The events that shaped my life fell into two categories: the times I was existing and the times I was living. Outside of my time at Xenon where I felt like I was on top of the world, I was only existing each day. When I was back in the apartment with Kim, I was drawing the parakeet, dreaming about a different future.

The light inside of me kept hinting there was more, but I didn't know how to find it or get there. Graduation was supposed to bring me the answers, but instead, I felt equally lost.

I woke up in my seedy apartment. Got dressed. Walked to the bus stop. Waited for the bus. Hopped on to go to my shift at LaBelle's. Then it got only slightly more interesting (in a disturbing way) as I spent the ride avoiding the man who sat a few rows away, staring at me and openly masturbating. Then at the next stop, the man swinging a machete as though it was normal joined us.

The day the masturbator sat next to me while touching himself, the decision was clear. *I have to get the hell out of here.*

There's more for me. Somewhere. I'm ready to find it.

I knew I wouldn't stop until I found it.

I called my dad. "I need a car." I refused to take the bus again. Other than the six months I had my Fiat, I had depended on the bus or rides from other people. No more. I wanted that freedom back. And, I wanted to be safe. At least having a car would allow me to protect myself from harm more than I could now.

Dad took me to the car dealership where we looked at all the options.

I walked around, deflated. I stopped admiring the cars and only glanced at the price tag before moving to the next one. Everything was out of my budget. I couldn't afford a car, not even a monthly payment.

Dad saw my face fall quickly. "I went into the military when I was your age."

I cocked my head at him, wondering if I heard him right. "The military? What do you mean?"

"Yeah, they'll train you, and it's a job. You can join the Reserves or the National Guard and still be in Utah. It's just one weekend a month, and I bet it will be enough for a car payment."

The seed was planted and growing fast. I could do this. But if I did, I'd leave Kim high and dry on the apartment. That's not fair. I wanted to be a woman of my word and not bail on someone who needed me.

As soon as I walked through the door, I told her, "We need to talk. I think I may join the military."

Kim lifted her head from the magazine she was flipping through long enough to say, "I'm already doing that. I've already spoken to a recruiter."

I bit my tongue, fighting off the anger that swept through me. I didn't hop on my plans because I wanted to make sure was taken care of first. She was the first person I thought of, concerned that my actions would negatively affect her. It was the responsible and caring thing to do.

But Kim didn't have the same consideration for me. It

was a trigger for me. People doing whatever the hell they wanted to do and just leaving me behind.

I reminded myself, *no one is looking after you, Gina. You gotta take care of yourself.*

I booked an appointment with the recruiter and chose the National Guard as the next step in my path.

Training for a career. The ability to buy a car. That was exactly what I needed.

It was my ticket to finally get someplace else in life.

17

STARTING ANEW

*T*he structure of the military filled my desire for stability. If you do this, you can get this. Simple. Rewards. Consequences. Dependable income. Black and white rules. No guessing. Systems in place.

The process for entering the National Guard included taking the Armed Services Vocational Aptitude Battery (ASVAB) exam, a physical, and meeting with a counselor to determine a career path.

"You can request what you'd like to do. There's no guarantee you'll get it because they'll put you where they need you. But you can pick the top five areas that appeal to you based on your test scores." The potential to have options for my future thrilled me. I had to score high. I wanted choices.

The recruiter called with my test results. I was super eager to hear how I scored! He said, "Gina, we need you to retake your ASVAB."

"Why?" I was stunned. I thought I had done pretty well.

He didn't give me an answer, so I did as I was told and took the exam for a second time.

A few days later, the recruiter called again. "We believed

there may have been cheating involved when you took your exam."

My mouth dropped open. "I didn't cheat!" I protested, wondering where in the world they gathered such an absurd conclusion.

He laughed and agreed. "We see that now." The second scores were the same as the first. I tested very high in everything, and poorly in engineering. The score discrepancy activated a red flag.

I simply didn't understand how to build a bridge. *What does that have to do with anything?* At least I passed the academic and integrity tests.

"Based on your test scores," the recruiter continued, "there are a lot of things you can do. And, depending on which one you choose, you'll get to see a new part of the country. The tech schools are in a variety of places. What path do you want to take?"

"Where are the tech schools at?"

He listed off a few, including one that piqued my interest.

I had never been to Mississippi before, or even to that side of the country. I was eighteen-years-old. It seemed like a reasonable choice when I had nothing else guiding me.

"I want to go to the school in Mississippi," I replied

"Okay," the counselor continued as he scratched down my answer on a piece of paper. "Administration or Air Traffic Control are two great options based on your test results. You can do either one."

It only took me a moment to realize that being held responsible for the safety of airplanes seemed a bit crazy at this point in life.

"Administration," I confidently replied.

"Okay," he said.

And just like that, with a simple choice, my future was set in motion.

Within a week I was sworn in with my step-sister, Kim, standing right next to me. My dad and Ike were not happy that we had only called them the night before letting them know of our decisions and the soon-to-be-swearing-in process. (To be fair, it was my dad who planted the seed in my mind.) Kim, too, had chosen the Utah National Guard and would stay in Texas for her training to join the military police. We were both on our way to Lackland AFB in San Antonio, Texas.

Kim left shortly after our swearing in, and I followed two weeks after her. I flew out to the Lackland AFB with no idea what I was doing. I was excited and happy Kim would be there, someone I could go through this experience with.

The first week of basic training was a shock to my system, to say the least.

"Stand here. Walk now. Halt!"

"Don't look that way, look at me!"

"Salute Airman!"

"Left, left, left, right left."

I was being screamed at constantly, which I didn't handle well in the past. But this was a different type of screaming that didn't trigger me in the same way.

I absolutely loved it.

Don't get me wrong, it was the hardest thing I had ever done. I had never exercised before, but I loved the release of endorphins from challenging myself to do things I never would have tried before.

Most of all, I loved the structure.

The military made life easy to predict. If you do this, then this happens as result. It was a system of actions and consequences, of right and wrong. No gray areas here like I had struggled with my entire life. If a person messes up, they get recycled, which you *don't* want! Each week was built around learning the next steps. A person had to prove that they were learning and progressing. Failing at any point was a fast track to being recycled back to the prior week. Relearn it, prove that you got it down, and you can move on to the next week. All a person had to do was stay within the lines. I had eighteen years of practice with that.

The military laid out the expectations, taught the systems, and ensured everyone was learning. That was the epitome of guidance I sought during childhood but didn't receive. All those times I looked to my mom, waiting for her to guide me, teach me. The military was doing it, filling a need deep within.

There was one simple purpose: to do your job while protecting yourself and your fellow airmen. If your leader yelled, "Go! Out to the front line now!" in the midst of a war, they wanted to trust that you'd go without hesitation.

I was willing.

As I acclimated, I realized not everyone in my flight was in the Air National Guard. Some were guard, some reservists, but most were full time active duty. Everyone was going through the exact same process. I wondered if Kim had figured that out yet. I saw her only once during my time in basic training. I was in formation marching down a path with my team when I noticed her standing at full attention on the side of the path. She was alone and waiting for our group to pass. Interesting. *Why isn't she with her flight?* I would later learn she had been recycled and was on her way to her new flight. Our eyes met as I marched by, I nodded only slightly so as not to be reprimanded for pulling out of formation.

In the last week of basic training, we were challenged to

complete the confidence course. Our final test to be able to leave this place and start our military careers was twenty-seven obstacles to challenge our physical and mental endurance. You could fail only three obstacles within the course before being recycled and forced to stay another week to repeat the entire grueling course. There was one thing I was quite sure of: I could not and would not get recycled.

The day of the course, I was terrified and ready, determined to finish. The anticipation of what was to come sent electricity in the air as everyone warmed up and stretched their limbs. Then it was time. I was off, running to the first obstacle. Success! Obstacle two—success!

The third obstacle was a long rope hanging down like you might see on a tire swing. It was draped over a pool of gross green water. I climbed on the platform, grabbed high up on the rope, and swung myself forward. In motion, my hands slowly began to slide down the rope. I couldn't hold on, and I fell into the pool with a splash.

My first fail. Twenty-three obstacles remaining. I couldn't let that happen again.

I pulled myself out of the water, my clothes heavy and soaked as I ran to the next one. Five wooden horses greeted me in various heights, some to jump over, some to slide under. I ran as fast as I could, planted my hands on the first one to push myself up and over it. The water from the pool had yet to dry, and I didn't account for that. As soon as my hands hit the wooden surface and my body lifted off the ground, my hands slipped. The rules stated that if you're in motion and don't find success on the obstacle, you fail it. I was not going to fail twice in a row. I landed on the wooden horse, hard. Straight down on my chest. Pain shot out in all my nerves, and I gritted my teeth to keep from crying out.

Only later would I learn that I had cracked my sternum. All I knew at the time was that I had to keep going.

I threw my leg over the horse and pushed my body to the other side, breathing through each movement as the sharp pains cut through me.

One obstacle after another, my muscles were shaking from the exertion, but I kept going, the finish line almost in sight. I was nearing the end. Five, maybe six obstacles away. The next one was a long rope draped over the length of a pool. I climbed on the platform, turned my back to the pool, grabbed onto the rope, swung my legs up, locked them tightly around the rope, and began to pull myself backward. This went well in the beginning. I had gravity on my side! I pulled my body across to the middle of the pool. Then I realized my body froze, hanging there, right over the middle of the water. My arms shook and my hands were too weak to hold onto the rope. I pulled my upper body up, wrapping my arms tightly around the rope trying to figure out how to scoot the rest of the way across the pool. The screaming was intense! "DEFA! MOVE YOUR ASS! YOU ARE STOPPING THE ENTIRE SQUADRON FROM GETTING ACROSS! YOU ARE GOING TO GET PEOPLE KILLED! MOVE YOUR ASS ACROSS THAT FUCKING ROPE!" I grabbed onto the rope with my blistered, bruised, and weak hands. Moving one of them back behind my head to pull myself backwards and up toward the platform on the other side of the pool.

That did not work. I fell into the pool with a splash.

My second fail.

The pain in my chest—not to mention my hands, legs, and arms, was so intense that I wanted to stop, but I was too close to the end. I kept pushing...and I finished!

I walked around afterward, high-fiving everyone else

who finished. Alive. Stronger than ever. Gripping my sternum when no one was looking.

I adopted a new belief that day. *If I can do this, I can do anything.*

THEN I WAS onto my next adventure! Off to spend eight weeks in tech school at Keesler AFB in Biloxi, Mississippi. I knew those eight weeks would go as fast as the first eight weeks did, and my stomach turned at how quickly this would be over.

Anytime I thought of leaving tech school and going back to the life I once had in Utah, I reached for a paper and pen to draw the parakeet as the anxiety rose. Finding a new apartment that was as rundown as the last one. Struggling to keep food in the fridge. Having to go back to riding the bus with the masturbator and the machete man. No. I didn't want any of that.

I could stay in the National Guard and do one weekend a month. It may be enough money to pay for a car. But I wondered, what's the point of going through all of this just to do one weekend a month? I worked hard; why not get the full-time paycheck and benefits?

Besides, I knew a long time ago, I didn't belong in Utah. I had a taste of what else there could be, and it fit me. It made me feel valued and like I was a part of something greater. I had a new strength.

Instead of allowing a moment of adjusting to the way things used to be, I decided what I would do. The day after I got back home, I walked straight to a recruiting office and said, "I want to go on active duty."

The recruiter pulled all my records to verify that I was good to go. "Well, I only see one problem. Your engineering test scores were too low. That one has to be higher to go active duty. You're going to have to retest."

Those damn engineering scores kept haunting me. Who knew they'd be so important?

I called my dad for help. His entire life was spent around construction. If anyone could get me through this next exam, it would be him.

Dad was on board, always ready to help. He took me to the library to pick out the books I needed. Then we went to the only place that made the most sense to study. A diner where we could learn over pancakes. He drew bridges on his napkin, while I drew a parakeet on mine. He took time explaining how structures were designed.

This time, I passed the engineering exam with flying colors. When asked about my preference for duty station, I chose the place Kim had moved to because I had nothing else guiding me. We had gone through this together so far, why not keep it going? Kim had met a guy in tech school and fell in love. Lew was active duty and promised to marry her. When he learned he would be stationed at Grand Forks AFB, North Dakota, Kim switched from the Utah Air National Guard to the North Dakota Air National Guard and followed him there. I was ready to be on my own, but I was also scared to do it all alone.

Within weeks, I was on my way to Grand Forks AFB.

At the airport drop off, my dad asked, "How much money do you have?"

I shrugged, gripping my bag closer. "I don't know. Twenty dollars maybe."

Dad reached into his wallet and thumbed through the bills, handing over fifty dollars. "You can't get on a plane and leave forever with only twenty dollars in your pocket, Gina. What will you do when you get there?"

He was concerned, which was sweet to see.

"Kim knows I'm coming. She said she would pick me up from the airport." All I could focus on was one step at a time. I didn't know what my life would look like by next week. One step at a time. That's how I had gotten through everything else so far, and it served me just fine.

I gave my dad a tight hug, knowing I would miss him terribly. I got on a plane and said goodbye to Utah for what I hoped would be the official start of a brand new, happier life.

18

BUILDING A LIFE

*N*orth Dakota is frigid. If you haven't been there before, let me be the first to tell you.

I shivered as I stepped out of the airport and took my first step onto the Dakota land. *What the hell!?* A few hours earlier, I had been standing in the Utah autumn breeze, a perfect calendar-worthy scene of the definition of fall. Now it was freezing! And it was Halloween. How do kids get to wear costumes and trick-or-treat when it's sub-zero temps?

Kim picked me up at the airport with the heat blasting and drove me straight to the hotel on base. I assumed I'd stay with her and Lew since it was Friday and I didn't have to report to my new squadron until Monday, but that wasn't the case. She dropped me off, and that was the last time I saw her for months. No invite to Thanksgiving dinner or any acknowledgment when it was Christmas. I was on my own. Cold. And on my own.

How quickly the plans dissolved for Kim and I to go through this next part of our lives together. I selected this base in hopes to have "family" around. I hadn't planned on staying at the military hotel. I hadn't considered how I would eat or maneuver alone without a car. I hadn't planned on the money needed to pay for the hotel, base taxi, or meals. Dad's fifty-dollar bill rescued me.

I sat in the hotel room drawing the parakeet as I waited for orders and watched the snowfall outside, trying not to think of this as a mistake. *You can only depend on yourself, Gina. Maybe there's a reason you're here and Kim was just the reason to make it happen.*

Per the instructions I was given, I called my first sergeant. "I'm here," I announced with all the confidence I could muster. Within five or six days, I was settled with a job in my squadron and a room in the barracks where I was staying with a roommate.

Kim's abandonment was the final straw to realize I had to say goodbye to all of Utah, including any hope that someone would walk next to me down a new path.

This life was mine to live.

I could do this.

I was a 702, which loosely translated to administrative work. I worked in the Base Forms and Publications office, filled with great big office rooms where all the regulations were housed and revisions happened. The military rewarded efficiency and proactiveness, two of my strengths. A perfect match. I fell into an easy routine in no time.

Winter came—apparently my first day experience was nothing compared to what was coming. It continued to be shockingly cold. North Dakota could be brutal.

Around this time, my first sergeant made an announcement, "I got orders and will be leaving. I have a car to get rid of. Does anyone want to buy it?"

I shot my hand in the air. Buying a car was exactly why I joined the Air Force in the first place! Could it be any more perfect than this?

Soon, I was the proud owner of a dark gray 1986 Ford Escort. I drove around, basking in the freedom (and the warm heat blasting through the vents). I no longer had to rely on anyone or go to the bus when I needed to get around. I could grab my keys and hop in my new ride—even if I didn't have any place to be.

But I also had to learn about car ownership and how to take care of it in the middle of the coldest winter I had ever been in.

A call to my hero of a dad and block heaters rescued me. He walked me through the importance of purchasing an extension cord with a special coating so that the block heater would keep my car ready to go when I needed to start the engine. It was one of the most expensive purchases I had to make. Apparently owning a car wasn't all about the pros with no cons.

Especially true when someone unplugged that expensive extension cord and stole it.

That one piece of equipment held more value than one may realize. It was my first costly purchase while learning how to fully be an adult that didn't include a roof over my head. It was my first time trying to protect something that I had earned. It was the first time I was trying to live and survive as an adult and learn how to do this on my own.

It felt like I had been stripped of something more than just an extension cord. I was angry. Really angry.

Then wisdom arrived from a coworker. "You have to plug in the block heater, put the cord near the tire, and drive over it so no one can steal it." Golden advice that was a game changer.

That's all I had to do, not just with the extension cord, but with everything. Continue to learn, apply the information, and survive.

Keep learning how to protect valuables like the extension cord.

Keep learning how to protect myself.

Keep learning how to grow and move forward.

This was life, and I was learning what I could.

My time was filled stepping into my new job role and making friends at work and in the barracks. I lived in the moment, truly enjoying the confidence that came from continued independence.

My supervisor wasn't a big fan of me, though. She was a tough cookie. I was highly capable and did as I was told, but she was determined to push me on even the smallest things.

It was the 80s, and I loved my big 80s hair. Big hair, however, was a big no-no in the military. A female's hair couldn't be more than three inches in bulk, couldn't touch our eyebrows or collar. So I would walk toward the office, pushing the beautiful height down on my head before I stepped through the door. SSgt R. would run toward me with a ruler to measure it. She was going to catch me with 3.5" hair if it was the death of her! Somehow I always managed to slip by.

There were not many women in the Air Force, and I had hoped SSgt R. and I could be friends. She pressed her uniform, styled her hair, and wore makeup while so many other females did not. Like her, I did. I liked to look nice. I liked to put effort into myself as I walked out into the world. I thought taking care of myself would attract others to me, the companionship I desired from the time I was a child— not have them chase me around with a ruler!

Luckily, I didn't report to her for long. I was moved to another area, just down the hall, and I was given a new supervisor, Sgt Doris King. Doris and I quickly hit it off. She was quiet, sweet, and thorough with a wicked sense of humor. Standing a few inches shorter than me, Doris had beautiful dark skin and her jet-black hair was always in a tight plat down the back of her head. She was married to Michael who was as outgoing as Doris was quiet. He was from Gary, Indiana and Doris was from Biloxi, Mississippi. They were adorable together and soon became two of my dearest friends.

The heart of downtown Grand Forks was about thirty minutes away. In the winter, that easy drive translated to thirty minutes of steering-wheel-gripping, death-fearing driving from the barracks that I avoided if I could. Thank goodness the NCO Club was only a short five minutes away. I missed Xenon and needed an outlet for dancing. I found it at the NCO Club! Every night after work, I could be found there, dancing my pain away. Every night except Monday nights. Trust me, I would have gone on Monday nights if I could, but it was closed.

My job suited me just fine because I could work and be rewarded. I was coachable, loved getting things done, and always strived to improve. That's the military training in a nutshell. I was happy there. While at work, I had to conform to everyone else—uniform, shoes, hair, no jewelry. The moment I got home to the barracks, I would throw on a dress, add heels and a few inches to my hair, and top it off with dangling hoops. Time to have some fun and relax!

There were many regulars that I danced with, a guaranteed man coming to get me for the next song. Despite twirling around the floor with them, it was the men who didn't dance that intrigued me most.

Especially one.

Tall, with a perfect mustache and beautiful dark skin, sitting at a table with a drink in front of him. He simply leaned back in his chair, not saying much, observing everyone around him, holding his chin as though he was silently dissecting the world.

The only problem was that he didn't dance. I would have loved a partner to spin me around daily. Still, I couldn't help be but be drawn into his reserved nature, the opposite of my big personality, more similar to that of my dad's.

This man stood out, dressed to the nines in European clothes. Tan leather shoes. Dark blue jeans that were ironed with a crease down the front. Colorful, geo-blocking sweater. Stylish. We would look good together.

I wanted to know who he was.

I started my sleuthing, asking everyone more about him.

My first revelation: the white Mazda RX-7 I had been admiring while equally shaking my head at the impracticality of it in the northern winters turned out to be his. Apparently I had a thing for Mazda RX-7s considering that was Randy's car as well.

Doris and I investigated and more information was revealed over time. The mystery man's name was Staff Sergeant Palmer. He had moved to North Dakota from Europe three months before I did. Those simple pieces of information immediately told me one big thing about him: he worked hard for the things he wanted in life. One of the most attractive qualities in a man.

After finally locating someone who knew him, I passed on the phone number of the pay phone down the hallway. "Tell him to give Gina Defa-a call."

I never waited for someone to come to me. I knew what I wanted when I wanted it, and I wanted Staff Sergeant Palmer.

Once the phone rang, we went on our first date, and many more followed.

For the first time, I didn't want to date anyone else. Everal, Ev for short, was it. All I thought I needed. Marriage was on my mind, ready for stability, and he was the right ticket. I took him to dinner at Doris and Mike's, and they approved as well.

About six months into our relationship, he received a TDY, Temporary Duty Assignment, to go to Saudi Arabia. This was in the late eighties so we didn't know what exactly was happening there at the time. All we knew was that it was supposed to be a three-month assignment, which was a long time for a relationship that just started, especially in military time.

Before Ev left, I asked, "Are we moving toward something or not?" He was six years older than me and had more worldly experiences. If I was ready, he should be by now. "You gotta figure out what you want while you're gone. I need to know this is going somewhere. I'm ready for the next step."

Ev had appealed to me because he had seen so much of the world already. His demeanor showcased it when he was sitting at the NCO Club. His choices and conversations reflected it afterward. I wanted that life too. I wanted to go places, experience things I had only imaged could be possible, hungry for growth and learning and life. The Air Force had given me a taste of it. I wanted more.

While Ev was gone, I drew the parakeet daily, trusting that everything would be okay. We had no way to talk to each other outside of a very expensive phone call once a month. I sent him care packages with letters every other week; he sent me letters with songs he wanted me to listen to in return.

The day after Ev returned, my greeting was straightforward, "What are we doing? Are we moving forward or not?"

It's safe to say after many years of not speaking up, I had found my voice.

Ev wavered only ever so slightly before saying, "Yes, I think we should get married."

I kissed him and with a smile announced, "Good. I already found my engagement ring." Like I said, I don't typically sit around waiting for things to happen.

Once we went to Zales, I pointed to the one I had picked out. A cluster of eight small diamonds surrounded one in the center like a flower that sat on a thin gold band.

"This?" he asked, surprised at the selection.

"A flashy ring for a flashy lady," the saleslady emphasized with a smile. She got me. She knew.

Ev bought the ring with only minimal hesitation. He took it out of the bag and asked, "Do you want to put it on now or not?"

"Is that your proposal?" I fired back.

"Well, we already agreed to do this, right?"

I just nodded and held out my hand. On a July evening, he slid the ring on my finger. We decided that the following May would be our wedding month.

But life doesn't always care about our calendar plans.

A few weeks after our engagement I discovered I was pregnant. Doris, found out she was pregnant, too, only days after I had. On top of it, Doris and her husband had just received orders to go to Japan and were leaving in October.

I turned to Ev and pleaded my case, "We can't get married in May. It's important to me to be married before we have a baby. And I really want Doris to be my maid of honor."

I didn't have many people I could depend on to be a part of my wedding and Doris was a non-negotiable. Kim and Lew had married and moved to Italy, so she was gone. I was too scared to tell my dad and stepmom I was pregnant and getting married, so they didn't even know. "I don't have any family here and you know Doris has been like a sister to me. What do you think about September?" I asked, pushing the calendar in front of me toward Ev.

Ev let the words soak in before slowly asking, "Like, next month?"

I bit my lip, watching the downslide of his reaction. "Why does it matter if we're getting married now or in May? Isn't it all the same? The only difference is Doris won't be here if we wait."

Ev avoided eye contact as he relented with a shrug. "Okay."

We married and moved into a little apartment in Grand Forks. Ev worked in the missile field, which meant four days away each week while he lived in the underground area guarding the silo. My baby bump was growing and I was settling into a nice routine of working and learning how to be a wife. I didn't like the nights Ev was away, but he would call each night and wish me sweet dreams if he could. Each time the phone rang at night, I jumped. It was either him getting off his shift trying to catch me before I fell asleep, or it was my mom. She became a sloppier drunk over the years, and somehow meaner still. She wouldn't ask how I was, but would call out of the blue to sling insults and judgments.

"How much do you weigh? Do you weigh more than me?" Her gritty, smoker's voice echoed on the other end of the receiver. She didn't know I was pregnant.

All these years, I had accepted my mom as my mom. She was an alcoholic and mean. It's all I knew.

But my life was changing. I was taking back control. I was going to create a life for my baby that was better than the one she gave me. I would love my babies, protect them, and prove to them every day that they are seen and heard.

"Are you ugly now?" she pressed.

The ghost of my mom could no longer haunt me. For the first time in my life, her words bounced off me instead of permeating my being. I found my voice and said the words I should have said a long time ago, "Listen, you cannot call me anymore if you're going to talk to me like this. I have a life that I'm responsible for. I will not allow you to disrupt that with these calls anymore. If you want to get clean, I'm here. I'd like to have a relationship with you. But until you stop drinking and clean yourself up, I'm done." Taking a deep breath, I said, "I have to get up in the morning and I need sleep. Do not call me again unless you're ready to get the help you need."

I hung up the phone and cried as I drew the parakeet with one hand and rubbed my growing belly with the other.

19

PLAYING HOUSE

*O*n May 1, 1989, I left the military. I had served three and a half years. I didn't want to leave, but a choice had to be made. Ev and I couldn't risk both being deployed. We were not willing to leave our new baby with someone else to raise her, even for a short time. Ev had been in the Air Force six years longer than me and had more rank, so it was decided. He would stay in, and I would get out. Technically I had another two and half years left on my enlistment, but there was a clause that allowed early discharge due to pregnancy. That was the first decision I made as a mother, choosing the needs of my baby and our family over a career. It was scary. So much of my self-worth had been restored and my hope in the future renewed while I was there. But I drew my beloved parakeet and trusted everything would be okay.

A month before my twenty-second birthday, I delivered a healthy baby girl who we named Monica. Doris delivered her son Max three days later. They were in Japan and we kept in touch with letters throughout the years. I loved having someone I could navigate motherhood with and that

Monica and Max would grow up knowing each other, even if it was from a distance. I had a sister in Doris and could provide Monica with a "cousin."

Holding this baby girl, the doubt of being a mother rushed over me. I didn't know what to do. I knew what not to do from my own raising, but I didn't know how to make it all right. How do I do better than what my mom did?

I can't mess up my daughter's life. Everything has to be perfect.

While some instincts would kick in, relying on the innate fact that I was doing okay in the day-to-day process of raising a child was nonexistent. I wanted to trust everything would be fine. But it didn't work that way, which only made me feel more incapable and anxious that I could mess it all up. I was frantically scratching out the parakeet every time I was alone with my own thoughts.

Monica was almost a year old when I was ready to go back to work. I had to do something that I felt confident in, and motherhood made me doubt myself more, feeling as though I was sliding back into my past. I went to the local workforce office to see what was available. There was an opening at the insurance office where Ev and I had our policies. Every time I had walked into that office, I felt a sense of peace. It was that light within guiding me. When I saw they were hiring, I knew that was the job I wanted. They were hesitant to hire me at first since the facts were obvious: Ev could get orders to move at any point and I'd have to go with him, but when their first hire fell through, they offered me the job anyway.

As much as I loved my administration job in the Air Force, the insurance industry just naturally clicked for me. Within two weeks of starting, I was explaining difficult concepts to potential clients and delving out advice as though I was a seasoned pro. I knew I had landed on something that would serve me for years to come.

I was in a nice groove for about nine months before Ev received orders to leave. We were relocating to the Netherlands. Ev had been stationed there before moving to North Dakota. He knew it well, which was comforting. He would work at a NATO base, which hosted military from six nations. Only about 300 American military members were stationed at our tiny Dutch location. A natural fit for Ev, but an adjustment for me.

Monica was only two-years-old, and I was consumed with learning how to be a mom and take care of her. Even after two years, I struggled. I doubted every move I made in motherhood because I didn't want to do it wrong. I didn't have anyone to share my insecurities with, and Ev was not helpful. He didn't understand why I was so worried about getting this right. Something as simple as hosting a birthday party for Monica would send me into a tailspin. I never had a birthday party. I had no memories of ever attending a child's birthday. I wanted everything to be done right but had no idea what "right" was. Everything had to look and operate perfectly as though this one event could scar her for life.

When we moved to Holland, the freedom I once sought by being able to move around freely was removed again. There was a six-month required waiting period for family members to get an international driver's license. We lived far away from the base where Ev took our one car each day, the 1986 Ford Escort. He resented that I made him get rid of the RX-7 when Monica was born. It was like tearing his heart out! So here we were with the Escort that would peg out at 85 mph on the Autobahn. The dashboard would shake, and we would drive with one hand on the wheel and one on the dash to try to keep it from shaking so much.

I was at home with Monica, alone, in a foreign country with no other Americans around me, and no car to get anywhere on my own without the structure that I craved. Before the move, I had felt like I was beginning to build my life, to learn how to thrive and not just survive, and now here I was, alone most days and feeling extremely incapable of raising this child.

Ev listened to me, but he shrugged it off. "Everything will work out, okay?" He attempted to throw comfort my way as he walked out the door. He had to go to work, I needed to get it together, I needed to figure it out. Easy, in his mind, but it wasn't reassuring.

Figure it out? I felt like someone had dumped all the parts of a jet engine in front of me and told me to put it together without any directions and with my awesome (not!) skills in engineering. No pressure, it just has to be completely safe so a pilot can jump in and fly above the earth's atmosphere. Good luck!

Any wonder why I started slowly breaking down?

As time went on, it became evident I was being triggered in ways I couldn't fully comprehend. Something as simple as going to the grocery store could threaten an anxiety attack. I avoided cans of Spaghettios, Sugar Snaps, Captain Crunch, and bologna. Those foods I ate alone in the dark nights of waiting for Jack and Mom to come back for me. I didn't think about how they made fears, apprehension, and loneliness rise within, I just avoided them. "No Spaghettios for you, Monica!" If I don't buy it, I won't see it. If I don't see it, I won't have to feel the pain of not being enough for my mom. I thought controlling that was healing. Controlling it by pushing it away. Getting on with life. Taking care of my responsibilities.

Apparently it doesn't work that way with deep scars. If only I had known back then that deep scars needed triaged differently, something I would go on to learn twenty years later.

The environment forced awareness of my weaknesses on deep levels. There were so many lights shining on me, revealing every bit of dirt and ugliness that I couldn't remove or hide. The past was haunting me regardless of how much I tried to avoid it. I could no longer escape to a job or to my dad to fill the void.

I had to face things head on.

In a very isolated way.

I once thought life was on a pre-determined trajectory that everyone set out to travel. Graduate high school. *Check.* Get a job. *Check.* Get married. *Check.* Have a baby. *Check.*

But then what? I checked all the boxes, but I didn't know how to do life. I had no answers on what to do next—other than throw away all the alcohol in the house. I did that. No alcohol was allowed. I was not going to grab a drink to calm myself. I didn't know if I would become an alcoholic, but I knew I was not going to take any chances.

I would choose differently than my mom.

However, my anxiety levels were rising more every day. I finally reached out to my doctor and got a recommendation to a therapist. Ev was supportive, but as usual, didn't react much. He didn't try to help me. I was going to therapy. I was doing all the things I was supposed to do. But there was no emotional comfort. I felt alone, as always.

I knew God was still there. He had me. My faith was

strong, but it was battling with deep-rooted emotions I had yet to deal with from my childhood. Somewhere along the line, I jumped on a boat and floated down a dark hole. Within a couple of months, my anxiety had murdered my appetite. I wanted to sleep all day. When I was awake, my thoughts went into overdrive, shouting my failures at me just like in basic training, hanging over that pool, desperately trying to hold on to the rope. The pill bottles were stacked like the Leaning Tower of Pisa. Anxiety medication. Depression medication. Change the dosage. Try a new medicine. Cycle repeats.

My therapist finally recommended something different. "Let's try an in-patient hospital." Relief flowed through me. There was my escape from all the things I wasn't good at—being a wife and mom—to get some help.

One problem: I was fairly stranded on a small military detachment in Europe, the medical care difficult to reach. I was put on a medevac plane, which is similar to being on a bus. It flies from one military base to another, picking up and dropping off passengers. Flying only added to my unease. They heavily medicated me before putting me on the plane. First stop Frankfurt, Germany, next Naples, Italy, and next, somewhere in England. By the time we landed at my stop in England, I was completely out of it and barely aware of how to move one foot in front of the other to get off the plane. A car was waiting to pick me up and deliver me to the mental ward.

I don't remember the drive, but I remember walking into the facility declared my haven for the next two to three weeks. The horrendous smell greeted me first. While waiting to be processed in, I stared at the bulletin board with the daily schedule of group therapy and meal times. My eyes struggled to focus enough to read the board. A person approached and stood next to me, staring at the board just like I was. I looked down at the short and stocky frame with dirty blonde hair with a bowl cut that had me debating whether they were a boy or girl. They had ice blue eyes that reminded me of Jack with freckles. A strong, feminine voice answered my question. "Welcome to the fucking nuthouse," she said.

My eyes widened, suddenly more sober. *Maybe I'm not supposed to be here. A fucking nuthouse? I just need help being a mom.*

The woman looped her arm in mine and told me she was my roommate as she proceeded to take me down the hallway to our room.

I was to report to group therapy within an hour after arriving. It was 9:00 pm, and I was exhausted. They fed me and sat me in a chair that was one of ten chairs formed in a circle. Folks started wandering in, sitting down, picking at the scabs on their wrists. Evidence of their recent suicide attempts.

Yeah, really not sure I need to be here. What have I gotten myself into?

I soon discovered my roomie, Ruth, was not "crazy" but she wanted everyone to think she was. She nicknamed herself "Crazy Ruthie." She was in the Army and had been assaulted by a male soldier who was going to show her how great it was to be straight by "fucking the gay right out of her." Ruth went AWOL the next day and when they found her hitchhiking a few miles away, they brought her back and told her to get her uniform on and report for duty. She told them what happened and the response was, "Sounds like that soldier did a good thing for ya, Ruth. Why would you want to be gay when you have all these men around you?" So Ruth became Crazy Ruthie at that exact moment. Now she was my roomie, and I was grateful the stars aligned for us. Another way God was protecting me by keeping me tied to the truth of my circumstances, a rope that I clung to so I didn't sink.

Ruth had been at the facility for months with intentions to either stay there with her new name or receive an honorable discharge from the United States Army. As far as she was concerned, that was up to the Army to decide. Ruth shielded me from the dangerous patients and educated me on the shortcuts, which would help me get the resources I needed. I soon went from being in the "general suicide prevention" sessions to being in the adult children of alcoholics and sexually abused sessions. I was learning how to process the trauma, and I was teaching Ruth how to draw my parakeet. Healing was happening for us both.

Two weeks later, I had to say goodbye to Ruth who was staying behind. I was put on the plane with fewer drugs, headed back to The Netherlands. I was still terrified that I didn't know what I was doing as a mom and wife, but also very confident that I did not belong in the psychiatric hospital.

20
___

THE TRAIN

I split into two people coexisting in the same life. One Gina was growing more confident in who she was, going to therapy to work through her trauma, soaking in another culture, and learning a new job. On the outside, she looked like she had her shit together. But the other Gina still felt overwhelmed, dissatisfied, a failure at being a woman. I didn't know what to do daily at home, and no one would give me a black and white description. I needed it to be made clear. Like a job with a performance review so I could be told what I was doing right and what could use some improvement. Every professional job I had felt like second nature. I wanted motherhood to be second nature, but instead, I was swimming in cloudy water, searching for affirmations I would never find.

Sometimes the best thing a wife and mom can hear is, "You're doing a great job." Many of us are secretly pleading for someone to speak the words we long to hear. Even a, "We will get through this together" would suffice. But there were no reassurances, nobody saying, "You've got this. I'm in your corner if you need help."

Ev's lack of response to how I was feeling created a massive crater between us. I needed to figure out how to improve my marriage to Ev. How to feel better about being a family. So I made suggestions like going on family walks, attending church services—anything to bring our family closer and bond, but Ev refused to partake.

I was constantly working on myself, on a mission to feel perfectly capable at all roles I took on in life. Learn and improve what wasn't great. Fix it. Whereas Ev felt automatically proficient and never saw the gaps that existed in him or our marriage. I couldn't tune out the glaring problems like he could. I wanted the holes filled with the love, respect, and communication that should bridge two people together in a marriage. I wanted all the things I wasn't a witness to for most of my life.

"I'm a girl raised by my dad. You're a guy raised by your mom. We should be able to cross-reference and get all this right. We should be able to come together and hit this out of the ballpark. Two halves make a whole, right?" I wanted it fixed. I wanted us to be a unit.

But Ev remained quiet, to himself, unwilling to admit deep-rooted insecurities or strive for a higher version of what we had the potential to be. He was calm, status quo, chill. That was fine when we were dating. Building a family and a life, however, required a bit more of an emotional investment.

I no longer felt close to him, and after struggling for many years, I finally found the words to say what was on my heart. "I want a divorce. When you get orders to leave, we'll go wherever that is. I'll find a separate apartment, and we'll be there when you get there. I won't keep you from Monica, but I don't want to be married anymore."

In a surprising move, Ev refused to succumb to a

divorce. Instead, he offered to give us space. He moved up to an attic bedroom as a temporary solution.

I wanted to live my life. I wanted to grow. I liked my work and my continued growth toward learning how to do this mom thing. I was calm and so much more at peace when I could just be my truest self. Ev felt like the death to it. I was planting grass seeds and watering them daily, while he was spraying herbicide because he didn't want anything to change.

Then the voices inside started. *Are you really going to give up on your marriage, though? This is what you wanted. Marriage. Kids. Stability. Now you have it. So what's your problem?*

Oh, the voices of doubt were ever present. "It's good enough. Why complain? You really think you're worthy of more?"

Ev and I had been going around in circles with the same conversations for five or six years. It was always me saying, "I need you to show up for us," begging him to do that. He tried. I believe that. I also believe that, like me, he didn't know how to do it. How to be a dad, a husband. He didn't have that example on a daily basis either, but couldn't admit that he didn't know what he didn't know.

My do-it personality screamed, "We need to fix this. NOW!" Ev's personality countered with, "Eh, let's just sweep it under the rug. Don't talk about it. Don't make it an issue, and it won't be. Let's watch TV. That'll make it all better."

The day Ev received orders to go to Minot, North Dakota, he begged, "Please. Just give us another try. Let's go back to the states together. I will try harder."

I relented, and we stayed married.

We left The Netherlands the first week of June. Two weeks later, I learned I was pregnant again.

As we settled into our new home, I found another job on base. I was excited to be in a new position, adapting and focusing on this next phase of our life together as a family.

A few short months later, my first ultrasound showed I was having twins.

Expecting a regular appointment that I would be in and out of, it quickly turned to me not going back home.

"There's a problem," the doctor disclosed. "We have to admit you. We need more tests."

The results of the tests soon resulted in an immediate medevac flight to Write Patterson AFB in Dayton, Ohio, hundreds of miles away from Ev and Monica. "We can't care for you here. Your pregnancy is very high risk. You need more specialized care."

The anxiety that I had recently worked hard to keep at bay suddenly rose in my throat as the unknown presented itself.

There turned out to be a lot of problems, not just one.

Two months alone in a hospital bed, states away from any family, with strict directions to move as little as possible, God's reminder of hope through the parakeet drawings saved me as I sketched on one hospital piece of paper after another. I tried to remind myself that I wasn't in a cage again, which was hard to remember when two, maybe three bathroom visits were begrudgingly allowed. If I needed more than that, I had to call for a bedpan. Even with a daily rotation of doctors and nurses examining me, running tests, and trying everything they could to save the babies, the prognosis was grave.

"There's a 4 percent chance both babies will live."

"There's a 11 percent chance one will live."

"Eighty-nine percent of the time they both pass away from the complications."

The time in the hospital was terrifying of course, but it also forced me to release what little control I had.

I had to truly let go and trust God.

Day after day, I lay in that hospital bed and ate every calorie they directed me to eat. They knew the twins would be born early, and if they lived, they wanted them as big as possible. I needed to eat, eat, eat in order to give them the best chance to grow. They didn't want me moving and using any of the calories—all of it should go straight to the babies.

For someone who normally likes to go, go, go, it was a forced time to slow down. A time to learn the importance of no longer wasting a day with trivial concerns.

I drew strength from remaining positive, a skill proven to lend itself in my protection through the years. I drew the parakeet too. He was with me almost daily.

The nurses would come in and have lunches in my room to escape from the heaviness of other patients. We'd joke and laugh and have a great time. My doctor surprised me one day while examining me. "There's a good chance you would have lost the babies by now if you didn't have such a great attitude."

Some days the sadness overtook me, but I stopped and considered that yes, I could be sad and feel sorry for myself. *Or* I could realize the only power I held was over my attitude and what I'm able to do to help the babies survive. That's all. Two choices. Bask in positivity to send out good thoughts to the babies, or sit in negativity and stew.

The decision was easy. A focus on mindset strength won.

Besides, this would be the last time for at least eighteen years I would be able to lay in bed and eat all day, so I may as well take advantage of it!

Five weeks in the hospital and twenty-four weeks into the pregnancy, I was told that Amara, the name I would choose for the first of the twins, was big enough that if I went into pre-term labor, she could possibly survive. Alissa, the second of the two, wasn't quite there. She wasn't big enough and they doubted she would make it even if she were bigger. Many of her internal organs couldn't be seen. Since she was most at risk, I was repeatedly advised not to bond with her. For two weeks, the doctor would come in each day and ask, "If you go into labor today, do you want us to keep you pregnant and jeopardize both babies or let you go into labor and try to save the bigger one?"

I wept from happiness the day they told me they felt Alissa was at least big enough to make it now. Still unsure she would live, she was 1.5 pounds now and that, they felt, was big enough to have a chance.

A week later, my two sweet baby girls were born three months premature, but very much alive.

TWO WEEKS before their original due date, the twins were released from the NICU. The three of us were loaded on a medevac plane that delivered us to Washington, while Ev and Monica packed up the house in North Dakota and drove to meet us at our new home at Madigan Army Medical Center in Tacoma. There was an Air Force Base next to the Army hospital that had the resources we would need to care for the twins. Ev had a job, and I was ready to be a stay-at-home mom who would continue making the best out of the life I was given. I couldn't work because the twins would need special care and therapy for at least the next three years.

With a lot of time to consider what family meant while I was alone in the hospital waiting on the twins' arrival, I consented that no marriage was perfect, so I vowed to focus on the good things with Ev.

I had a newfound mission to be present. That was all that mattered. I had to be there for the girls. I couldn't be focused on tomorrow. I accepted that life was not going to look like the fairy tale I had painted in my mind. Instead, my faith and gratitude would guide me every day.

I had no energy leftover to change things from how they were into what they could be anyway.

Three years passed quickly, filled with constant doctors, appointments, and getting Monica acclimated to having two little sisters. Finally, I had embraced motherhood and let go of expectations of perfection. I had three beautiful girls who were stepping into their own personalities, and I was so proud of how far we had come. As things calmed down internally and around me, the confidence in my ability to parent grew. I was ready to put an emphasis on my needs again and find a decent balance between work and motherhood. So, I returned to work in the insurance industry where I had already discovered a flow and ease with a purpose to help others.

My drive with raising my daughters was to give them as "normal" of a childhood as possible. I figured it out bit by bit. I was *doing*, I was taking care of things, I was stepping into my mission. It was more than just existing; I was living. This is what I had wanted during my childhood. No more survival. Truly living this life as it deserved to be experienced.

After ten years of adjusting to the valleys and peaks in life, learning who I was and growing more self-assured, I knew I could do more. I was ready. It was brewing within, bubbling to the surface.

My love for the work I did was perfectly aligned with my

strengths, so it only made sense to start my own insurance agency as the next step. It was a wonderful decision! I felt empowered by helping others. I was challenged on a daily basis, always on the hunt to absorb more knowledge.

Ev and I coexisted together. We parented and ran the house together, but we were not a unified unit. Very little conversing happened that had nothing to do with the kids.

By this time, Monica was a senior in high school and the twins were in sixth grade.

I had settled into this life. Every day was predictable. It was comfortable.

Then one day, out of the blue, the switch flipped again when least expected.

A customer handed me a piece of paper and said, "I feel like I'm supposed to give you this."

I opened the paper to read the contents, taken back by the story inside. It was about a man riding a train. The train's purpose is to take the man straight to his destination. But in life, that destination is death. So along the way, the train stops at different points to showcase all that the world has to offer. Does the man just sit in his seat and look out the window as an observer as it (life) all passes by? Or does the man take a chance and get off at a stop to explore the possibilities of what could be waiting for him?

It hit me like a ton of bricks.

The message was clear.

God said, "It's time to get off the train."

So, I got off the train.

Ev and I got divorced.

It seems shocking that God would suggest that, doesn't it? I will probably lose several of you with this admission. That said, it was the hardest decision I've ever had to make simply because I didn't believe it was what God would suggest either. Yet, it was. God wasn't the one who told me to marry Ev. I did it without asking. It was time to move forward with a new life and staying in my marriage was not going to allow me to do that.

A new season of life was blooming.

21

EXTENDING FORGIVENESS

*W*hen I turned fifty, I began to really look at the early years of my life, I saw a lot of darkness. People. Times. Circumstances. Events. All simply dark.

As I have stepped into my own individuality, showing up as my truest self, the light within grows stronger. There were times, like those anxiety-stricken points of being a young mom, it dimmed a little. But mostly, the light has grown brighter and brighter. It had always been a part of me, but I didn't know it when I was a little girl. I just followed my instincts for survival. Now, I can see it for what it was. Not just in me, but in everyone I meet.

When I see darkness competing with my light, I will step away. I won't allow it to enter my space—my head, my heart or my home. These are sacred, and I have worked hard to build and embrace each one. Chaos cannot enter. Peace. Calmness. Love. All the things I didn't have as a little girl. I'm fiercely protective of those things now.

The divorce from Ev was a rocky time, and an adjustment for us all. I continued to work hard at my business to provide for my daughters. I moved up the corporate ladder and into leadership, fueling my passion for helping people. My girls grew into beautiful young women. Their father had his own struggles and distanced himself from them. While they talked to him occasionally, it crushed me to witness the break in their relationship. Already one with deep-seated abandonment issues from my own raising, I carried guilt about it being my fault for far longer than I should have.

I had to learn how to forgive myself. I also had to learn how to forgive other people.

While in the Netherlands, working through therapy to find healing, I called Jack. I wanted to get his perspective on the events that took place when I was a young girl. It took several times of me calling and asking the question, just to have him hang up on me over and over.

Jack and Mom didn't get married right away, but when they did, my mom was wife number four or five on the rotation. Jack had five or six kids; they were spread between all of the wives before my mom.

Then there was me. Not his blood, giving him permission to use me however he wanted. I'm not sure which one would have been worse, being his blood or being a target of his free-for-all advances. According to Jack, I got the better end of the deal.

One last phone call, I finally cornered him, threatening to turn him in. I had checked; the statute of limitations was not over. I ensured he knew I would have his ass thrown in jail if he would not simply talk to me, give me some answers. I demanded, "At a minimum you owe me this!"

Jack knew that, so he finally gave in. He confessed that when he met my mom, he had promised himself that he would never hit her or me. Apparently, with his ex-wives and his kids, he had beaten them all. He knew that was the truth to why those relationships ended and why several of his kids wanted nothing to do with him. He also admitted that he was beaten as a kid and struggled to break the pattern. So when my mom and I came into the picture, he vowed to never hit me. The closest he ever got was when he spanked me after I was busted for stealing the latch hook at the drugstore. Before he did, he had said, "This will hurt me more than it will hurt you." Famous words that now struck me for what they were. They held a deeper meaning than I realized at the time.

There was an odd peace that came from his reasoning. Jack didn't know what he was doing. He was acting and reacting as to what was normal to him. He truly thought he was doing better than what he did with his other kids. He was trying. That didn't excuse him from what he did to me, but it gave me insight into what he was thinking. It was enough for me to forgive him. Jack would never harm me again. There was no sense in letting it consume me.

Besides, the molestation was never the part that hurt the most.

That said, it was nearly impossible for me to forgive my mom.

Everyone has a backstory, which has shaped who they are today. Jack had his story, even though I may never know all the details, it shaped his racist, womanizing, controlling ways. My mom had her backstory too.

My mom's dad was also an alcoholic. It was too bad for my grandmother, who was fabulous and worthy of so much more, which thankfully, she got later in life. My mom was the youngest of five kids and a witness to the worst demons in my grandpa. She never told me the stories, and if she would have maybe I could have understood her more, to be able to see things from her eyes and her perspective and how it affected her after all this time.

Instead, I had to hear the stories much later in life from my aunts, like how my grandpa lined all the kids up against a wall, screaming and waving a gun, threatening to shoot each of them.

I imagine that would scar anyone.

Grandpa's alcoholism was so bad that he crawled drunk into a boxing ring. The boxers were in the middle of a full-blown match. Standing up, my grandpa teetered with his fists up, as though he actually had a chance to fight one of them. He got punched in the head and that was it for him. He fell to the ground and remained bedridden, lying in a hospital bed in my grandparents' living room, until he died a few years later.

No matter one's history, people have the choice to either take their past and set out to make sure they live better than that, or let the past control their future. The choice is ours. My mom, for reasons I don't know and can only surmise, chose the same demons as her dad. The alcohol kick started it all. Her daughter didn't matter as much as the escape in the bottle of Black Velvet provided. When Jack came along, her worth became wrapped up in him. She was nothing if he wasn't happy with her. It's easy to see how that pattern could have started when she was a little girl.

I saw it reflected in my desire to be loved and seen.

When I look back on the early years of my life, the worst part wasn't Jack touching me, it was my mom allowing him to do so. It was her ability to leave me alone for hours, for nights, for days. No communication, no idea when she would be home. It was her refusal to keep me safe, hammering the belief that my worth was nonexistent. Over and over again, turning her head from every motherly responsibility, from every chance to show me true love throughout my life. I had a long list of grievances with her, but the neglect was at the top. The abandonment first stripped away any security I felt as a child, slicing deep scars that I still carry. Those were the ones that affected every relationship I had in life. All from her consistent actions that screamed I wasn't worth her time.

By 2008, I had an established career in the insurance and financial services industry. I was living in Bloomington, Illinois with my girls by my side. My story was still unfolding in amazing ways, and I was learning how to heal one day at a time. The past kept trying to pull at me, though, attempting to suck me back into the darkness I worked hard to escape.

A small envelope arrived with my mom's loopy cursive handwriting on the front addressing it to me. My aunt must have given her my new address. I noted the return address and my stomach cramped. Joplin, Missouri. The next state to Illinois. Jack and Mom were close by. How did this happen? How did we both end up in the Midwest from Utah?

I opened the envelope and pulled out the folded contents inside. It was an obituary announcement for Jack. Nothing else.

I sat down with the paper in my hand. I read over the announcement, not feeling any sadness for myself. I felt it for my mom, though. They had been together at least thirty years by then. I wondered how she would go forward without him. I hoped he had passed peacefully, and at the same time, I was glad he was no longer on the planet.

Death forces you look at things square in the face. I was sitting in my bedroom looking at Jack's face and reading his life story while only a few hundred miles away from my mom. She had just lost her best friend. So I said a prayer. Then I grabbed my grocery list and headed out to get on with my day. Part of me wished it would not have been like it was between us. But it was, because of the bad choices they made and the cycles they couldn't seem to break.

Now that I had her address, I started sending her annual Christmas cards. No note, just a photo card of my daughters and me. Random cards from my mom also began to arrive in return. A birthday card simply signed with *"Mother."* A poem my grandmother had written without a note, just the poem. Random items at random times. I dreaded opening them each time but couldn't avoid the curiosity to see what was inside. The hope always existed, now an aged wick, but still with a desire to catch flame, a real mother-daughter relationship, the hint of something pure and good within. She was a part of me; I was a part of her, despite everything that filled the broken crevices between us.

I opened the newest package from my mom, wondering what random item she sent this time. Inside was a jewelry box, dingy, antiqued faux leather with a gold filigree design in each corner. The broken latch was taped down to keep its contents contained within. I recognized it immediately. I remembered the red velvet that lined the inside of the box and knew that when opened, the top of the box would pull up a shelf that held earrings, while the bottom would be filled with necklaces and stick pins. Jewelry that I used to sneak into her room to play with when I was a child.

I picked at the tape and released its seal. From the moment I opened it, the smoke and scent of bourbon filled my nostrils, taking me back to the memories I had tried hard to forget. The shiny faux gold chains with gaudy flowers attached, the white daisy earrings with a yellow bead attached in the center....memories of standing in front of her bedroom mirror as I tried on the jewelry while she and Jack cackled at the TV down the hall. My breath caught in my throat, a panic attack threatening. I slammed the lid down and shoved the jewelry box back in the packaging and hid it under my bed. Covering my mouth with my hand to try not to vomit, I hurried away from the box. *I'll open it another day. I am not strong enough right now. Maybe one day I will be.* Proof my mom had no clue the damage that she caused. Why did she send this to me? Was she being kind by sending it, or was she trying to rip my heart out? I never knew with her. I never knew what her motives were.

Six months later, a letter followed. Scrawled out in dark ink, I read her words. "You ungrateful bitch. You've never changed. I sent you my mother's and my great grandmother's jewelry and you couldn't even send me a thank you note? You are nothing but a little bitch! You have always been ungrateful! I am done with you. You will not hear from me ever again. I don't know why I even bother with you. I'll have someone call you when I die."

I fell to my knees. I was forty-two years old, crumpled and crying on my kitchen floor. She had gotten to me. Even after all this time, she could crush me.

I don't know why she bothered with me either if I was always a disappointment.

Mom was true to her word, though. I never heard from her again. I continued to send her an annual photo Christmas card out of obligation. Twelve of them, all answered with her silence. I wonder what she did with them.

I WAS INVITED to attend a small group at Church in 2019.

"What's the topic?" I asked my friend.

"Forgiveness," she replied.

My mom's face immediately crossed my mind. "Nope.

Ask me to the next one. I'll make that one instead." *I see what you're doing, God. Nice try. I'm not giving in to that.*

There was only one person in my life I hadn't forgiven, and I was at peace with that. I had been dealing with over forty years of various forms of abuse from my mom. I didn't need to forgive her. I could let go and move on without having to address it.

Apparently, God blocked my memories of saying no, because next thing I know, I was walking into that small group meeting. I had completely forgotten what the subject would be that night. As soon as I was reminded of the topic, I dropped my head. I couldn't really leave at that point, so I had to go with the flow.

Around the room we went, each person asked if they had someone they needed to forgive.

No, I don't. That was the only thing stubbornly racing through my mind. God pulled at my heart, trying to convince me that wasn't true.

When it was my turn, I admitted out loud, "Well, there is someone, but I don't want to forgive her. I'm truly good not doing it. I'm okay. I don't need it." I turned my head to the next person, waiting for their answer on forgiveness.

The leader had different plans. "Let's talk about that, Gina. Who is it, and why wouldn't you want to forgive them?"

Ugh! Thanks, God. "It's my mom, and it's too long of a story to share here."

The leader launched into a full explanation of the importance of forgiving before it's too late. "What if she dies? How will you feel?" *Blah, blah, blah.*

I shrugged my shoulders. "I'll feel fine. I'm totally good with my decision." I looked at the person next to me again, raised my eyebrows and nodded my head, implying a very forceful intent of, *Go ahead, it's your turn. I'm not saying anything else.* Lips locked. No one was getting anything else out of me. My decision is made. Period. Queen of Stubbornness and okay with the crown. No one knew what I went through, so how could they counsel me without knowing the details?

God was still at work, though. The small group conversation— including all the things I thought I successfully blocked from the leader's mouth—continued to sink in after I left. Two weeks followed of God softening my heart. *Maybe I could. Maybe I should. Maybe it's time to move forward.*

Exactly three weeks later, I received an email at work from Kevin, one of Jack's sons from a previous marriage. "I hope it's okay to email you here. I had to Google you and this was all I could find as a way to reach you. I want to talk to you about your mom. She's really sick."

Kevin? *Oh, I forgot about Kevin. How do you forget about a stepbrother?* He even stayed with us at King's Row one year. We saw our first movie together, *Star Wars.* How did I not remember him? Anger bubbled up inside of me. I have so few memories from the first thirteen years of my life. Other than the horrible things, my mind is blank from that time. It's incredibly frustrating that I lost part of my life and now talking to Kevin, realizing I didn't remember him was all I could think about.

I have to shake out of this fog...listen, listen to what he is saying Gina.

I listened and immediately, the skepticism kicked in. I haven't heard from Kevin for forty years and now he is calling to tell me my mom is sick. Why call me? What am I supposed to do about it? I figured he was trying to get me to send money, so I thanked him for the call and hung up. I didn't want to think about the ugliness or be reminded of the childhood I lost.

God continued to whisper to me. *Forgive. Forgive. Forgive.*

And I ignored, ignored, ignored.

A month later, I got another phone call. This time from my mom's sister. "Your mom is dying," she said with a shaking voice. *Here we go again! Where have you been for the past fifty years, Aunt Joy?*

The devil was whispering in my ear, *yeah, where has everyone been, Gina? They only call you when there is bad news or when they want something. What are you supposed to do about this? Do they need money or someone to take care of her?* Shaking my head again to clear the anger, I asked my aunt what the doctors were saying.

The cigarettes and alcohol had caught up with Mom and lung cancer staked its claim. She probably had it for years but never went to the doctor, so by the time they found it, it was too late. She wouldn't be coming home from the hospital.

The last time I saw my mom was nearly twenty years prior at my grandma's funeral. I didn't know it would be the last time, but even if I did, I'm not sure I would have done anything different than what played out. A brief hello was exchanged as she and Jack passed by me. No more acknowledgement than that. Her mom had died and we were there to mourn the loss. Sadness had washed over me as I watched Mom walk by, though. *What about us? We are still here, mom and daughter.* I couldn't imagine this kind of broken relationship with my own daughters. I had thought about taking a step toward them to say more, but then Jack smiled at me, and a chill shot down my spine. My mom continued to look straight ahead, away from me, like always.

By this time in life, I rarely thought of the pain my mom

had caused except when she sent me those random packages. But I constantly thought of the kind of mom that I had grown into. I proved it was possible to be a good one despite how I was raised. I had mourned the death of my relationship with my mom for thirty years before the phone call about her cancer. I lost her when I was eight-years-old when she chose a sinful party lifestyle over her family. I mourned her again the night I told her I could not have a relationship with her until she was clean, which never happened. The attachment to her died long before she did.

I had two choices when my aunt called to tell me of my mom's impending death. I could either listen to the devil, hold onto my hurt and hang up the phone. Or I could really dig in deep and listen to the message God had been sending to me. I chose God's message. It was time for true healing. Not just to ignore what had always been, but to embrace it by looking at it straight on. "Tell my mom I forgive her, and I wish her a peaceful transition." As the words came out of my mouth, I felt God wrap himself around me. Then the lightness came. Peace.

My aunt returned to the line, "I told her and she nodded her head. Gina, a tear slipped out of her eye."

The next day I received a call from the coroner, informing me he had been given my name as Georgene's next of kin. I was the only one who could sign the death documents. He went on to ask if he could email those right over for me to sign. He was in a rush to release her body to be cremated, and my quick signature would really be appreciated. No one had called to tell me she actually passed. Only the coroner and only because he needed something from me in order to do his job. Again, the devil whispered, *no one cares about you, Gina.*

I carried that lie around for a few days before telling the

devil I would no longer believe him. Instead, just as I forgave my mom, I would forgive my aunt and everyone else who has hurt me as well. I accepted this life just as it is. With all of the brokenness, the hurting people, and with God's love to guide me through.

I took a deep breath, and as I exhaled, the tightness I had been holding onto began to subside.

22

HEALING

*L*et me take you back a few months before my mom passed...

In December 2018, I sat in a crowded field house at Illinois State University anxiously waiting for my last daughter to graduate from college. My oldest daughter graduated from Washington State University six years earlier. Another daughter, the identical twin of the daughter I was there to celebrate, walked across the graduation stage just six months earlier. Attending graduations, though not a new experience, filled me with just as much excitement for this daughter as I had for the other two.

Yet, something different happened at this one.

As Amara ran up the few stairs with a big smile on her face, a determined gait as she crossed the stage and stood in front of the gentleman who would transfer the well-earned document into her grasp, her arm extended as though in slow motion.

The moment Amara's hand wrapped around her diploma, I heard a voice faintly say, *you are done...you did it.*

What? Go away! Amara is on the stage! This was the time

to focus on Amara, not anything else.

But the voice was persistent. Softly, he repeated, *you are done...you did it.*

God. It had been a while since I stopped long enough to hear His voice. Still, I thought, *odd timing, God. Can we wait to have this conversation later? I mean, Amara. Is. On. The. Stage!* While I was arguing with God and trying to stay focused on Amara, I also realized at that moment that I had never considered what "being done" would feel like. Or that "being done" could ever even be a thing.

I'm a mom, are you ever done being that?

As you've read, I had spent the past thirty years trying to figure out *how* to be a mom. How to raise these three girls to be the very best versions of themselves. To give them the best start in life I possibly could. I simply wanted to do better than my mom did to me. I was determined to break a pattern of chaos, abuse, and hurt.

When I heard those words, "you are done... you did it," I was confused. *I'm still a mom, that alone means I am not done, right?*

God whispered, *right...and wrong. You will always be their mom. That will not change. You have done the work I asked you to do here. This chapter has been good. Now it's time to pause, rest, and just be for a moment. There is more work to do, but now you need to heal.*

I wasn't sure what that meant, and I was confused by the need to heal.

Regardless, the page still turned.

A release happened, and it happened quickly. I watched my daughters, all three of them, blossom. They were, indeed, good to go on with their lives. They are beautiful beings that make a difference for others, including me. My daughters claimed their adulthood and suddenly we were like friends, hanging out together, talking about life, grabbing dinner and enjoying each other's company!

It didn't happen without surprises, though. During this time, all three started seeing a therapist, mostly for anxiety and general adulting fears. I can't remember which one said it, but it came out something like this, "Mom, you know we are all in therapy because you never let us be sad. Or mad. Or angry. Or even have a bad day."

I was shocked, and admittedly, a little hurt. I had tried so hard to be a good mom! Every day it was the most important task I had.

Then I thought, *wait a minute. If being positive and always finding the silver lining is a bad way to parent, I am cool with that! Go to your therapy girls—be exactly who you are supposed to be! Talk it out, live it out!*

But I knew they were right. I had been hell-bent on being positive and forward thinking while raising them. I wanted them to know they could do and be anything they wanted to be.

I was proud of who I was and where we were as mother and daughters. Despite battling the constant doubts, fears, and anxiety, I had broken a pattern of abuse and had raised three empowered women. I had a successful career and my reputation was one of truly *seeing* and empowering others. So on this December day in 2018, when Amara walked across the graduation stage, God's message to me was not what I expected.

Rest and heal.

I didn't expect God to tell me to pause on taking steps forward, and instead, take steps back into a time I thought I was supposed to leave behind. I was unsure where to start and even more unsure it was something I wanted to do.

Two months after that graduation ceremony, I was in my

community group being forced to look forgiveness in the face. One month later, my mom died.

Is this what you were talking about God?

When I first decided to go to therapy back in the early 90s, I assumed it would make a small tweak in my thinking. I simply wanted the therapist to tell me how to do life right to ensure everything and everyone would be okay. I wasn't interested in dealing with my past; I was focused on the future.

That was enough for that time.

Now here I was, thirty years later not realizing how much emotion I would have to work through, how much I had compacted throughout the years.

I soon found myself sitting in front of a new therapist a month after my mom passed, telling him about my life, when he nonchalantly says, "Oh, you're a runner."

Offended, I squared my shoulders and said, "Runner?! I guess so—if you call running toward success, positivity and happiness, *running*, then sure, okay." (Insert eye roll here.)

He smiled gently and said, "Whenever you are ready, we can get started. It's time to sit with the pain, anger, disappointment, and loneliness. It's time to face the past and release each emotion that has rooted itself deep within you."

I was taken back by his suggestion. "You want me to go home, sit on my couch and think about all of the hurt, pain, anger? To feel sorry for myself? That is ridiculous. Not to mention...I don't have time for it!"

I truly thought it was an unreasonable idea, and I *really* didn't want to do it. I didn't want to go back and relive the pain.

But I did.

I looked straight in the eye of the ugliest lie the devil had told me. A lie I had believed since I was eight-years-old. A belief that I was not worthy of being loved. I had convinced myself that only my actions would qualify me as worthy. That on my own I would never be enough.

I didn't want to admit it. I didn't want anyone to know how deep my scars were.

Never did I think I would share my story in such a vulnerable and public way.

Yet, here it is.

And guess what? I no longer believe the lie! I now know I am worthy of love...just as I am.

God loves me. He carried me through—He's got me, every step of the way. I have persevered with grace. His grace.

Just rest, He says now. *Trust me.*

I trust Him.

I had set out to break a pattern, raise my girls, and have a good life. It wasn't easy. I wasn't perfect. But, I achieved that goal. I continue to heal and move forward. For you, the reader, whatever it is that you are going through, know that you are not alone. There are people who have gone through what you have. There are people going through it right now, just like you are. There are resources for you that were not available for me. Be sure you take advantage of them now if you need them.

Knowing what I know now, here is what I would say. Trust yourself, run to the light inside of you, follow your instincts. Find your parakeet drawing. Maybe it's painting an owl or a flower. Maybe it's exercising or cooking. Perhaps it's writing or painting. Whatever it is, go to it and let yourself believe you will be okay. Have hope! Let it in. Find someone to talk to who can help. I can't tell you how many therapists I have had, but each one has helped me move toward the next level of healing. They can help you too. Therapists, Pastors, friends and family. The key is to take the step of making the call. I am so glad I did!

Lastly, be the person who sees others. Share a kind word, buy someone's coffee, send flowers to the grumpy cashier at the grocery store. Remember, the man under the table took only a few minutes out of his day to change my life forever. Think about how you may change someone's life with one small act of kindness as well.

Stay tuned to me as well. There is more to do, of that I am sure. I trust there is more love and adventure coming my way. I will continue to share my journey, trusting it unfolds just as God has planned.

Nino and I continue to move forward, together, no longer caged. I invite you to come with me!

Gina today with her daughters.

Look at the birds of the air; they neither sow nor reap not gather into barns, and yet your heavenly Father feeds them. Are you not much more valuable than they?

— MATTHEW 6:26

RECOMMENDED RESOURCES

If you've experienced trauma in your life. I hope this book gives you encouragement in moving forward. You have a story, you have a "why"—you were put here for a great purpose. If you're still in the valley, continually moving to avoid the pain of your past, I encourage you to speak with a therapist and go through the powerful journey of healing.

I'll save a spot next to me where you can sit and take a deep breath, finding peace in simply being.

I'll even show you how to draw a parakeet.

If you are a child of an alcoholic, you can reach out to:
Adult Children of Alcoholics 310-534-1815 or
https://adultchildren.org/

If you have experienced sexual abuse, you can reach out to:
RAINN (Rape, Abuse & Incest National Network) 800.656.HOPE to be connected with a trained sexual assault provider in your area

Department of Defense (DOD) Safe Helpline designed for sexual assault services for survivors and loved ones:

1 (877) 995–5247

ACKNOWLEDGEMENTS

First and foremost, all glory to God for holding me tightly in the palm of His hand! For His voice which guides me throughout my life. He was always there, He knew me even when I didn't know Him. He picked me up, shook me off and has consistently pushed me back out into the world with mercy, grace, love and gentleness.

For Phani Aytam who created the Multi-Cultural Leadership Development Program (MCLP) which gave me a safe place to share my story for the very first time. For many *really early* Tuesday morning coffees with Phani and Brian Cunningham as we talked MCLP business and life in general. You two set my heart free during those coffee meetings.

For Sandy Bentley who I shared the story with as I prepared to tell it to the class. She didn't bat an eye, told me it needed to be shared and I would be just fine doing so.

For Doris King, Shelli Opsal, Keisha Parham, Denise Younge, Marti Hughes, Marla Wachter, Karen Wakefield, Christi Houser and Julie Vigil for their friendship. These women each scooped me up at different times in my life, loved on me and cemented my understanding of the value of Girlfriends.

For Jody Wilson, the best leader I have ever had. For encouraging me to share my lens, always. For truly hearing, not just me, but all of those you lead. You make the world a better place.

For Aunt Jeanette and Aunt Lynette, my dad's sisters, who put band-aids on my scraped knees, calamine on my chicken pox, always sharing words of wisdom and encouragement to be strong and to move forward.

Dave Rodriguez, MA, LMHC, for getting my attention by telling me I am a runner and stopping me dead in my tracks, all so I could begin to heal the most broken part of my spirit.

Lauren Eckhardt for the encouragement, belief, coaching, and pure tenacity in pushing me toward telling my story. For the hundreds of hours spent crying, laughing, crying more as I dumped it all out and we put it on paper and brought it to life. For trusting it is meant to be here to help others, just as I trust it is. Thank you, thank you, thank you!

ABOUT GINA DEFA

Coming from a home filled with alcoholism and abuse, Gina Defa knows the grit and grace it takes to not just survive, but to move into a life filled with peace. Her immediate instinct to follow her intuition (which she calls her light) has been the catalyst to every success she has been blessed to experience. Her greatest passion is to help others find and trust the light inside of them—no matter their past. Gina lives in Olympia, Washington with her two cats, Annie and Sophia.

www.GinaDefa.com

Made in the USA
Coppell, TX
17 November 2020

41530268R10120